## TO MY FELOW MEN OF THE SAILESMEN COSTUME JEWELRY ASSOCIATION

It is you my dear Brotherhood of the Costume Jewelry Sailesmen association that has given me the Aspiration to wright about my Life and also of the Costume Jewelry . . .

With out your help—and with out your kindnest and with out the respect you have givin me oll of this years that I have been with you, I dont think that I would be in the position to wright that Book.

God Bless my Coligs of the Costume Jewelry Sailesmen Association.

Thanks.

I Sami

## TO THE WHOLESALER OF COSTUME JEWELRY OLL OVER THE LAND

My dear Wholesalers and associated Frends that God has given me stranght of oll the years to be with you. You Mr Wholesaler is responsible for my Sucses. It is you my dear Frends that has given me the stranght to carry on of my late years and given me the oportunity to do bussines oll of oll my years.

You have olways given me respect as a Sailesmen and as a Men when ever I came to see you.

In conclusion Thanks—Mr Wholesaler.
God Bless You.
I Sami

# I, Sami

a memoir

## Sam Silverman

Illustrated by Jeremy Blatchley

ACADEMY

CHICAGO

Copyright © 2016 by Academy Chicago Publishers
Published by Academy Chicago Publishers
An imprint of Chicago Review Press
814 North Franklin Street
Chicago, Illinois 60610

ISBN 978-0-89733-742-7

The Library of Congress has catalogued the hardcover edition as follows:
Silverman, Sam, 1892–
    I, Sami: 65 years on the road.

    1. Silverman, Sam, 1892– 2. Sales Personnel —
Biography — United States 3. Selling — Jewelry
I. Title
HF5439.32.S57A35 658.89'6883'0924 [B] 78-15726

Cover design: Jonathan Hahn
Cover illustration: Jeremy Blatchley

Printed in the United States of America

*to my children*

# MEMORIES FROM MY HOME

I was born in Russia, city of Pinsk, state of Minsk. As I was growing up I stardet to understand the life of my Mother and Father. My Mother, highly edjucated and understandable . . . My Father was a good men but not edjucated. In fact my Father lived in a smoll villedge about a hundred miles from Pinsk. He was rased up without any edjucation. He could hardly sighn his name. My Mother was rased in Pinsk wich the city Pinsk was considerd full of bussines and lots of scools.

My Mothers Father was *rebai* but very poor. As time got along my Mother became in years in fact around 25. This days a girl of that age was considered a old maid and naturly Match Makers tryd to mach up for her to get married. But thos days if you haven got a diary (money to give to a felow) no matter how Beautuful the girl could be—No Soap. No Money No Wedding.

They didnt look for edjucation or good looking. Money, Diary, was the main subject.

My Mother wasnt bad looking. A fair complection. Little bead on the stout side. Not to tall, not to small. In fact if I could be an artist I could paint her face. There was no Picture of her.

*i stardet to understand*

7

Well, heer comes in the happines to Mothers life.

Oll of a sutten a Match Maker comes in to my Mothers home and tells the story to my Grandfather (his name was *Shachne*).

—Reb *Shachne*, we have a *chosen* for your daughter. (That mins in English a youngmen.)

—Fine. Lets hear it, replaid my Grandfather.

The Matchmaker stardet to relait about this young men.

—He lived in a vilage a hundred miles from heer. He lives with his perents. There is a Family of five. Two daughters, one son. I want you to know that boy is honest and kind. And olso a Go Getter. He works with his Father there. And dooing bussines in fish. Chickens. Butter and Eggs. Off course he is not as edjucated as your Daughter. And he is a couple of years younger than your Daughter is. . . . But remember, your Daughter is considered in years. It is not so easy to get a metch for her. And dont forget. No money. That is the maine thing. Reb *Shachne*, the Matchmaker said, thank about it. This is a wanderful opertunity for your Daughter. She is getting a fine boy. Edjucation put on aside. But a leaving he will make for your Daughter. Reb *Shachne*, let us bring the boy in to your hous.

In this day the Perents is the one to deside the Marridge, not the childrn. The perents are the Judge. That is the way things were in the 1800s.

—O.K., my Grandfather Reb *Shachne* said.

In the same time he turns to my Mother and said

—Tonite the Matchmaker will bring a felow for you.

And from that day on my Father fell on love in her.

And he notised there is no money and very poor. He began bringing in the haus from the country where he lived, Chickens. Eggs. Butter. Fish. Cheez. He was very good nature in hart. He new immedietly there is no money for a Diary. In this days the boy suposed to get a Diary. No metter wether the

8

boy liked the girl or not it was up to the boyes perents to demend money from the girls perents. That was the Costume.

Yet in my Fathers case he was himself maid the Dessision. So it went.

In the olden days.

My Mother on the other hand notised that my Father was very much illiteral. He could hardly sighn his name. No ritting, no writing. He had no scooling. Not Yidish and not in Talmud. My Mother. The Family maid the dessision for her to merry this boy.

The Father of my Mother said to her.

—*Brochele*, you are a girl in years. To me he looks pretty good. He will olways make a leaving for you. He is good nature. And as far as Edjucation, you will stard studying with him to read and wright.

And so she desidet to get maried . . . And my Grandfather stardet preparation for the Weading. . . .

My Father broght in Chickens Fish and som other Goots. My Mother on the other hand stardet to teach my Father reading and writhing and finaly they got merried.

My Fathers name was *MOTEL.* Mine Mothers name was *BROCHE.* Mine Mother was hiley edjucated. As they were going along in life my Mother was dooing up oll the contracts for my Father. People from the City useto come to her for advise and making contracts for others. Her reputation was so highley that even rabeis useto come to her and lissen to her dessision. . . .

We were six childrn in our Family—four Brothers, two Sisters.

Louie was the oldest. Jannie was the second. Harry was the third. Isreal was the forth. Sera was the fifth, and Sami was the sixth. That was my name.

6 children

My Mother died at 52, in fact young. Died from Pennysides. Thos days the doctors didnt know very much of that sicknes Pennesides.

My Father remerried one month later efter my Mothers death.

I will never forget the night before my Mother died. I was a little boy about eleven years old. She coled me over to her sick-bad and she said to me

—My chield, I am going away from you. And in time you will be growing up a young bussinesmen. I am leaving you a *Will* that in many cases you will be making deals with people. Your word should be the *Will*. A pise of paper, a contract you can tere up. But your word from your mout can not be tur up.

I keep this Will to this day. I hardly wright contracts. My promis is a Promice.

# ‹2›

## MY BROTHER LOUIS AND OTHERS

Efter my Mother died, the Family of six stardet to move on to America. The first one stardet with Louie. He was the oldest. He came to America and stardet to bring over one by one. He was very kind and good harted. He was the one that helpt out every one on us. One by one we came.

Efter all the childrn came, my Brother Louie broght over my Father and his wife and he was the one that stardet my Father and opend up for him a fish store. My Fathers second wifes name was Leah. She wasnt very smart, but a good wooman. People useto ask him.

—Reb MOTEL, waht maid you to merry this wooman?

His enswer was olways that he did it so he should not forget the intelegence and smartness from his first wife. But som times he said

—I saft a son by getting merried.

That was becos my Brother Louie went in the Russian Army. A year later war broke out betwen Russia and China. They wore redy to send my Brother to the front. And that was the reason for my Father to get maried one month later efter my Mothers death. My Father got a Diary from his second wife. 700 Rubel. And I remember very well with this money my Father paid off some Politisions in another city and saft my Brother Louie from going over to the front in the war.

In the army

Leah gave burth from my Father a little girl Lina so it became seven childrn in the Family. Lina lived with her perents until she got meried, lived a nise life and razed two nise daughters.

But I must bring back my Brother Louie. He escaped and left for America and before long he helpt to bring over the rest of the Family, including the Nelson Family—my Mothers sister *Chane* with her entire Family. He helpt everybody. I will tulk more about my Brother Louie and his wife later.

My Brother Harry also escaped from the army in Urop. He was little bead on the selfish side, but he was a good student, a good Father and Husband to his Family. He workt in the Metrpolitan Life Insurance but at nite he went to scool to become Dr. In the maintime he met up with a young lady Heln. Got maried.

When he gradjuated Dr. the Family made for him a big party. Efter we were oll selebrating and leffing, my Brother Harry got up to make a speech to the Family. He said

—My dear Family. To nite I am a Doctor.

Wich naterly we oll knew and aplauded him leffing. Then he said

—To morrow I am a pants manufacture.

Wich was to us a big surprise. He had olredy an arengment with a partner in a factory to make pants and he went don-ton the next day and stardet working. The partner worked inside and Harry went on the road with the pants. And you know whoet? Harry maid a lot of money. Becos in thus days whoet did a Dr get? ¢75 for a house coll, $1.00 tops. But as a Bussinesmen Harry's name became knowing oll over the Country.

He was the fonder of the Sholem Alaichem Folk Shule and useto write manny times in the Jewish *FORWERT* artickles. He was bringing his three childrn up to the Highest Edjucashanel standard. He himself and his wife Heln workd together for one Couse, to bring up Jewish childrn in the Sholem Alaichem Scool. That was thair gole.

My Brother Isreal was good nature but olways Poor. No bussines ability. But good harted. There agen Brother Louies help came in often to him. Louie opend up several stores for Isreal in repairing and cleaning sutes. But no metter whoet he tried nothing helpt. Israel had three daughters. He died a young men.

The fifth one of my Family was my sister Jannie. Jannie was olso intelectual. Went lots to opera, and was belonging to vereas organizations suporting Hechting. She was difrent from the rest of the Family. Little bead on the meen side. Not good nature. Selfish. She was making a leaving from Dressmaking. Later she sold dresses in her home. She got meried olso to a interlectual men. He never was a good provider for his Family. Never worked too much. He didnt have much to say in the Family. My Sister had this hebit to knock her husband regardless whoet he said. It was olways the opposite with her. She had three boyes with him and she razed them up in a fine menner but her personal life was no where.

*Little bid on the meen side*

14

Tonight i stand before you as a
doctor....

My Sister Sera. We the Family rased her and send her to scool. She hardly ever workd. We the Brothers helpt her in every way. She was good nature but she medup with a young men and oll of a sutton she got married with out our consent. Not to long efter she divorsed him for no support. She had a son by him. A couple years later she remeried to another men. By trade he was a cigar maker. Again she finds another *Shlimazel.* Never maid a leaving. My Brother Louie opend up several stores for him to make custom make cigars but No Go. By him she had two childrn. One nite oll of a sutton her husband dissepired and until today no one could find him. My

another shlimazel

Brother Louie gave her merchandise from his wearhous to sell to make a leaving for her Family. She worried very little and olways had a smile on her face. But she lived a lonely life until she died a young wooman.

So much for my Sister Sera.

always a smile on her face

# ‹3›

## MY BROTHER LOUIES MARIDGE

My Brother Louie got maried shortly when he first came over. He got maried to a girl from Pinsk. Her name was Sophia. One of the aut standing girls from Pinsk. Edjucated and had a good hart like my Brother Louie. At that time Louie was a cap maker. That was his trade in Pinsk.

I as a little boy was at that time at home in Pinsk. I remember when we got the good news that Louie is getting meried. The day of my Brothers weading my Father maid a Selebration in Pinsk. It was a regular dinner for the entire two families. Our famile and my Sister in low Sophies famile. But with out the Groom and Brid. We put ther pictures on the table. It was beautuful.

Efter the wedding my Brother and my Sister in low fixed up a little appartment but together workd very hard to make a sucses for thair life. Befor long my Brother quit his cap making and opend up a grossery on Rooswealt Rd and Leflon St. Oll it was on thair mine is to bring over one by one from ether side of the Family to America. They sucsidet and we oll came heer. Nothing was to hard and they sherd with oll of us.

Sophie had a helping hand to the entire Family. She maid room and maid us filling goot at home. The apartment was small but by Sophie was lots of room. The dor was open for Everbody. Every Friday nite we had to have dinner by Sophie. Espacialy on a holiday was no qwestion. Everybody was by Sophie. She was kind and good and good wart for everbody.

Sophie belonged to vereas Sosiadies such as the Hadassa. The Ort. Outside of this she was the orgenizer off the *Ladies Pinsker Aid Sosiadie.* She herself helpt personally to bring over from Pinsk and settle in America 35 orphans. She razed oll the money for that. She Sophie maid picknics in Milwaukee woods in the summer time and rented halls to make entertainment oll for the *Pinsker Ladies Aid Sosiety.*

My Brother Louie worked with her together. He provide oll

Everybody was
by Sophie

the reffels for oll of the affairs so they could make money for the organizashon. Both of them gave a helping hand not only to the Family but to strangers alike. In the main time they razed a beautuful family, three sons. Isidor, Jack and Charles or Chuck. Isidor gradjuated Law Scool and then took over the leadership of the family bussines, the Silverman Jobbing Co. Jack was an enjener and Chuck workd in the bussines.

Sophie died many years before Louie. Oll in oll she was a good wife, a good Mother and a good Sister in low to the Family.

Louie died in 1972. He was 92. The three boys of my Brother Louie oll maried and are leaving a respectful life with their familie.

# ‹4›

## MY BROTHER LOUIE AND THE NELSON FAMILY

Again I am bringing in my Brother Louie of his accomplishment and good dids that that men has done in his lifetime for his Family. He is the one that he is responsible for bringing over to America the Nelson Famile, *Tante Chane* and her intire Family.

Enty *Chane* was a Sister to my Mother so the Nelsons are 1st Cosins to us. My Enty *Chane* had seven childrn, five boyes and two girls. She had a hard time of bringing up her childrn. My Uncil Louie was a fine men but he hardly maid a leaving for the Family, and that was the time that my Brother Louie stardet to bring over one by one to America.

The first one he broght over the elder girl CHASHKE. Then the elder son Abe. Then my Uncil Louie. *Tante Chane* remained in Russia with her five childrn Leo, Ben, Hymie, Charle and Lina. Finely my Brother Louie sucsidet with hard ship and broght over the intire Family.

The rest of the five childrn were small and stardet scool in Chicago. My Ente *Chane* was very bright and kind. Good. She workd hard to bring up her childrn of the fienest.

My Brother Louie true a Politision got a soda water stand for my Uncil Louie on Rooswealth Rd and Sangamon St. At the stand he had Ise Cream, Candy, chuing Gum and fruit and 2 cent plain. And from that time on my *Tante Chane* and my Uncil Louie begin to see a little sun shine in thair window.

Oll the smoller childrn finish Publick school and hiy scool. As they got older they stardet to mix in Politics. Abe got true Politics a job of Bill Board Hanger. Charle helpt him olso. Then they som how got in to the Theatrical Bussines, aspeacily Charle. He was a Go Getter and a great Mixer with the Politisions.

First they sold tickets in the box office. Abe the elder Brother was English theatre and Charle was in the Jewish theatre. And

befor long Charle my Cosin has his own theater by the name the Lawndale Theater on Rooswealt Rd.

The two boyes helpt Leo and Ben to go to Colledge. Ben finish Law scool. And Leo became a great politician. He became a Commishiner on the bord of the liquer bussines. And Ben became a Judge in the Circut Court.

The credit is to give my Enty *Chane* for bringing up such a nise Family in a respectfull way. She was the leader of her family with her wisdom and smartnest. She had power to rich to the top.

Enty Chane

# ‹5›

## SOM MEMORIES FROM MY YOUNG DAYS IN PINSK

My Father was a contractor. His job was to pave the streets with cable stones in the city of Pinsk. He had his own large rafts, about four of them, and he had four people on each raft. He useto send them out to the small villeges to pick up from the farmers the cable stones. Each trip took about two weeks to go back and fort true the Canal and bring back to the city on this rafts oll the stones, wich my Father useto deliver to the contractor that paved the streets.

One day when I was in age not yet fourteen years old, my Father came to me.

—My son, I will send you to oll the villeges to by up som stones from the farmers, they should fill up oll the four rafts. Than you com back home as soon as you will accomplish that Mision.

He gave me expence money and seven hundred Rubils to make that porches.

The next morning I pact up my bag and I left. I rode in a hors and boggy to get out to the country. I was suposed to stay overnite at a willedge and the next day do the bussines and come back to Pinsk.

I went to a little inn in the willedge and hired a men to go oll around the countryside on a horse and tell the farmers that I came for the purpose to by from them stones and they should deliver the next day by wagan to the pier where our rafts are standing. I told the men to tell them I would pay for the stones depending on size and shape and haumany they broght.

Efter I had dinner I went to sleep. About twelve mid nite the landlady from the inn came in my room and woke me up.

—*Shachne*, she said, Get up.

—Whoet is it?

—You better get dressed. I have heard that oll around the country people know you are here with money to pay for the stones. Bad men from the country are coming here tonite to get your money. They will rob you and kill you.

She didnt had to tell me tweis. I got dressed in a big horry and she had one of her men with a horse to take me to the pier where our men was waiting with the rafts.

—You will be safe there, she said.

We rode up to the pier and our men took me and hid me in one of our rafts. I was safe.

In the morning oll of the surrounding farmers was bringing in by wagan the cable stones, of wich I paid them on the looks of the stones from 75 copiks to a rubel and a half. It depended on the value of the merchandise. There were a hundred copiks that time in a rubel.

By nite time oll the rafts was filled up with stones and in the evening we went back to Pinsk in the rafts. I came home safe and my Father got his merchandise. He said to me

—Son. You did a good job.

# ‹6›

## ANOTHER MEMORY FROM MY YOUNG DAYS FROM THE CITY PINSK RUSSIA

When I riched the age of 14 my Father stard thanking future for me, to make a *Mensch* for me. Finely he got an Idea that Fur business is good business. In Russia Fur bussines is the Aut Standing Trade. Fine. He happened to know one of the manufactures in the City. He went over to this man and told him that he would liked for his son to learn the Trade.

—Fine, that manufacturer said to my Father. Only on one condition. That you should give your son away for three years, with a contract and no pay. Then I will tich him the Trade.

—Fine, said my Father.

The Boss maid out a contract and my father sighnt the contract. And both of them shake hands.

*Mazel Tow.*

And with that my Father came home and said to me, Mein *Kind*, I maid a deal with the Furryer and you start tomorrow morning.

Fine.

The next morning I came to the Facktory. The Boss greeted me with a smile.

—Fine boy. If you will be a good boy, I shell learn you the Trade.

The first thing he gives me is a Broom—to sweep out the floor. Then he tells me clean up the working tables. Then when I finish, do some arrands for the Boss, the Bosses daughter. And what not. Even to take care of his Grenchild. Then late in the day he useto put me at the table to tich me someting little about the work.

The working hours was from eight to twelve, then go to lanch, come back and work til five. Go home for dinner and come back in the evening and work until 9 P.M. From Friday noon and Saterday is *Shabes*. You rest until Sunday. And that was going on for monts.

Finely one day, I said to the Boss, his name was *Shmoel Lazer*

—Reb *Shmoel Lazar*, when will you rally tich me the Trade?

He kind of liked it that I had the inishitef and wasnt afraid to ask him that he should do somting better than to do all kind nonsence. And he agred, and promised that he will take care of me and he will tich me better worke.

So I Sami tried my best to make good, and before long I starded to do Good Work. In one year I Sami was able to make almost a complet Job and the Boss was very happy with me.

Why not?

I do good work. And no pay.

In fackt he has got me yet for two more years to work for him, for the duration of my Father's contract.

Well.

I Sami stard thanking to myself, That wont go.

By that time I happend to find out a man that he was the orgenizer from the Furryer union. His name was *Yosil*. I went to his home. I introdust myself to him.

—My name is *Shachne*.

—Yes, *Shachne*, Whoet can I do for you?

—Yes, I shell relate to you my story, that my Father sold me to *Schmoel Lazar* the Furryer for three years. And my acomplishment, what I do in one years time, that I am making profitable work for the Boss and I am to work two more years with no pay . . .

—Good, *Shachne*, dont worry. I shell take care of this.

In one way he was toff and on the other hand he was also kind.

Then he said to me

—Dont tell your Father about your vizit to me. Go to work as usual. I will be ther in a couple of days.

Sure enoph.

*I shall give twenty four hours to decide.*

One morning *YOSIL* the orgenizer can in. When the Boss so him he got white in the face. He new immidiately ther is som truble for him. He says,

—Yess, *Yosil*, what can I do for you?

—Yes, *Schmoel Lazar*, I came for one purpis. To settle with you regarting your boy *Shachne.*

—Whoet do you want?

—This boy is making good work for you. And he is to work for you two more years with no pay. That wont go with me.

—Why, I got from his Father a contract. That is the deal we maid.

—Forget this, *Yosil* said to him in a roff voice. Ither you do my way . . . and you will do the way I want.

—What do you want? The Boss said to him.

—You give the boy three Ruble a week and returned the Contract to his Father or I shall take off Everabody from you Shop. And you know that I have the power to do that. I shell give 24 hours to deside and I will come back.

And with that *YOSIL* left.

In the evening I came home. We had dinner. Then I said to my Father,

—Pa. I have someting to relait to you. Don get engry at me.

And I tell him my story what prespiret in the shop.

For a minut my Father did not say a word to me. Then he gets up and slept my face. For a minut I was startle. But I took this respound as a good *kind* and with that I went to sleep.

In the morning having my brackfest my Father comes up to me. And I sure tought that my Father will spank me again for going over his hat and not to consolt with him.

Insted he came up and kissed me.

—I am sorry. I think you did the right thing.

The finale: My Father got back his contract and I was getting 3 Rubils a week. This ends my story in the 14 years of age.

36

# ‹7›

## I LEAVE PINSK

37

When I got to be in the age of fifteen, I starded to think about my future life. By this time my Brothers and Sisters are away from me in America. So I was alone in Rushia in my home town where I was born. Only my Father and Stepmother was left with me.

So I starded to wright to my Brother Louis that he should try to take me over to America and he should try to send me a ticket to come to America. In the olden days tickets and trasportation to come to Chicago cost about fifty dollars. Train. Hotel. Ship. And then train from the ship to train to Chicago. Finely my brother send me a ticket to come.

So finely I left home for America.

I shall never forget my trip. It was the most exsiding days of my life. In the hotel where we stayd befor bording on the ship I met up with a large group of wich I was asighnt to go with them to America. Amoungh that groop I met up with a yung couple.

The man from this couple was a *Rebai* . . . kinney olderly. The wife was kinney youngish. She, the wife took a liking to me. The *Rebai* was a little beet on the *Shlimael* side. I was at that time the life of the party amongst the groop.

I will never forget this trip as long as I live. DONT ASK. One night I got a bottle wodka and I got that Shlimael *Rebai* drunk. We sailed with the ship to America and I was wishing that we should sale for another two weeks. . . .

Finely the wonderful time that I had endet with good taist and I was exsidet to meet my family and arrive in Ellis Ighland.

38

the life of the party

# 8

## COMMING IN TO AMERICA. 1910.

I arived to this country in the year 1910 on March the 15. One of my cosins met me in Ellis Ighland—that was the low at that time that some of the relatives is responsible for the Imegrant to take him out from the ship. In the maintime my Brother Louie send five dollars to the Port by telegram so I should have some spending money for the trip on the train to Chicago. My cosin took me in New York. I stayd with him a couple of days and he showed me around. I was very imprest to see the great New York City. Finely mine cosin pact up a box lunch for me to eat on the train and put me on the train to go to Chicago.

It took 30 hours to go from New York to Chicago. I was admiring the stops at every station that the train stopped. The news boy useto bring up in a besket fruit . . . chuing Gum ... candy and sandwiches on every station. I couldnt understand the English Langwich but I got along the best I coud. . . .

Finely we arived in Chicago on Dearborn Street station. Ther on the station was my Brother Louie to meet me and he took me to his home. At home I mett for the first time my sister in low Sophie. She greeted me grashishly and maid me comfortable. At that time they lived on Rooswelt Rd neer Leflon Street in a jewish naiberhood. My Brother at that time had a grosery store in the front and in the back of the store they had three rooms. Bedroom, kitchn and a small parlor. With all of this small qwarter she maid me fill very comfortable.

The next day my Brother boght me som shirts, underear, shoes and dressed me up of wich I never had this kind of cloase before.

In the evening the rest of the Family came to see me. My Brother Harry and my Sister Jannie and som relatives . . . ants . . . cosins.

The Family stardet tulking to me whot I woold like to do and what kind of a job I shud look for. In the maintime my Sister in low Sophie said, Let him look around for him self and find the kind of job or trade to take up. In the maintime I said to my Family that I workd in a Fur facktory in Pinsk, Rushia, the city I came from and I was prety good in that line.

Then my Sister Jannie mentiond that she had a frend of hers, he is a manufacurer in Jewelry. She will ask him that he shuld give me a job in his facktory. The excuse from the Family was that I am too weak for beeing a Furryer. Lets get him a eassier job.

Finely I took thair advise and I went for the job in the Costume Jewelry facktory for $1.50 a week to stard.

I came to my Brother and told him that I got this job and all they will stard me with is $1.50 a week. My Brother Louis said

—Dont worry. To much we havent got. But food and sleeping qwarter you will have. You dont have to worry for the first three monts. You will not pay us anating until you will stard making more money.

And so I excepted.

43

I never had this kind of cloase before

In the facktory was two partners. Rubenstein and Agnion. Agnion was Itilian but very kind to me. They had a comb facktory. Making fency combs. I kinda liked this kind of work and I workt very hard to proof to the bosses my willingness to make goot on the job. This day we stardet to work at 8 a.m. until 5:30 p.m. Three quarters of an hour for launch.

Efter working 2 weeks my boss give me a rase $1.00 a week, wich I got oll redy $2.50 a week. I was very happy with that kind of rase. Efter the working hours I useto take a broom and clean up the shop and working table on my own Inishitive. The bosses kind of likd this for me working that hard. Especily the Itilian boss. He took a very liking to me. Before long efter working about 6 monts they rased me up to $5.00 a week.

Before long efter working 2 years I have lernd the Trade very well. One of the bosses tought me how to engrave on Combs and I became one of the best engravers and desighning all kind of sketches on combs. By end of the two years they rased my selery up to $25.00 a week. I became knowin amoungst the trade as one of the finest Desighners and Engraver in the laidies Hair Ornament.

We maid hair ornaments. Spanish Combs. Hair Pins. Barettes. This was the fondation of the Costume Jewelry. I liked that so much that I said to my self that som day I will becom the leader in the Costume Jewelry fild.

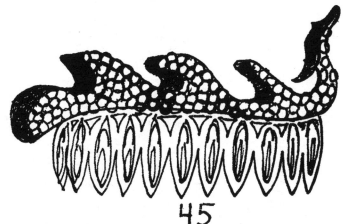

45

# ⸱9⸱

## CHEPTER OF MY FAMILY LIFE. FIRST MARIDGE.

As a young men I lived at my Brother Harry's house and I paid weekly for room Board. My Brother Harry was studing for Dr. Working as a life insurance salesmen dooing the day and at nite he useto go to scool to finish Dr. He worked very hard for a leaving. Of course by me staying in his home helpt him quit a beet. This day when I paid $15.00 a week that was a real help.

My Sister in low Hellen when she was not married she worked in a tie facktory. In that facktory there was a young girl that she was very fond of her and the young lady useto come in quat often to the house. But as a young men I never paid attention. I wasn't thanking of any kind of settling down. I was making good monney and had a good time. Thus days as a single men I was making $35-40 a week. It was considered as the best Income for a young men.

Well, one nite I came home. After supper Hellen my Sister in low, tells us at the supper table that Yetta (thats Hellen's girl frend) is sick at home. And she says to my Brother Harry that he should go over there to see her beeing that he is almost finishing for Dr. Perhaps he can prescribe for her to help her. That was almost 10 o'clock at nite. My Brother says to me

—Sami, com along with me. It is only 4 blocks from us.

So I get drest and we went over. . . . We came in. My Brother went in her bedroom, to egzamen her. She hed lots of fever. I pipt thru the door. I looked at her. She was beautuful. I will never forget her face. She was blusing from fever.

My Brother maid out a prescription to bring down that fever and ask who will go to the Drug Store to make this prescription. But no one could go, as she was staying with an old couple. By that time it was alredy 11 o'clock at nite. I jumpt up and I said

—I will go to the Drug Store.

I went. My Brother went home and I maid it the prescription and I went back to her house with the medicine. Then I went home.

The next day, after Dinner I went to wisit the young lady to find out how she is getting along. I did come in with a nise box of candy,

—How is our Pashiont? Filling much better?

MY PAYSHIONT

—Yessir, said the young lady to me. Filling much better. By the way, thank you for bringing my medicine to me.

—Very well. As long as you are filling better. May I come back to see you, my pashiont, again?

—I would like you to, replied the young lady.

By that time I replied

—I shell see you by end of the week. Good nite.

And I went home. Going on the way, I have been thinking about her. That she is a beautiful girl. There was something

49

about her that I felt from the first look at her that I shall come back to see her.

The next couple of days I coled her on the telephone.

—How do you fill?

—Fine. Much better.

—Fine. Glad to heer it. By the way do you have anything on Saterday evening?

—Nothing spachial.

—Good. I shell see you at 7 P.M.

I couldnt wait for Saterday to come, to see her. Finely the lucky day came. I stardet to get dressed in the evening. My sister in low Hellen askd

—Wher are you going so dressed up? And who is the lucky girl?

—Well, I replied, the most beautuful girl in the world and that is Miss Yetta Tyson, my Pashiont.

—Dont get to much involved. You are to young to be getting tied up, she replied.

That I dint like.

However I went and came in to Miss Tyson with a box of candy. She opend the door and I could see in her Ies that she was very happy to see me.

—How are you filling?

—Fine.

—Well, thats good. Are you redy to go?

—Just a few moments.

She went in her bedroom, got drest and we went out for the evening.

—Any particular place you would liked to go?

—Lets go and see a movie.

—O.K., I said.

We went to the movie in the naberhood. After the movie we went in a restaurant to have something in *nosharies* (that mins goodies). Sitting in the restaurant we became little closer and I stardet asking her about her family and from what part of the country she comes from. And I in returne have told her about my Family and from what part of the country we came from. By that time the evening got kind of late and I said,

—I think it is behind your bed time.

And we went home. On the way going home

—Did you had a good time?

—O yess, she replied.

—Would you mind if I come again?

—Yess. It would be my pleasure.

—Well, in this case I shell see you tomorrow Evening, and we will go to dinner. Will see you at 5.

—O.K., she said.

The next day, Sunday, in the morning my Sister in low said to me

—Did you had a nise time?

—Oh yess. By the way I will not be home for dinner tonite. I am going for dinner.

—With whoem?

That agin I dont like. But she is my Brothers wife.

It came around 5. I got dressed, went out and into a Flour shop. I got her a carsage and came in to her house. When she so me comming in with the Flour in my hand she became little startled, and teers came in her Ies. In this days a carsage ment a howlot by a girl. Just in that time I notised she became more frendlier, more worm to me and we went to dinner.

Naturley I took her to a nise place. Thus days when you paid $2.50 for a dinner that was the finest Musick, Wien and Densing. The everage boy in my years couldnt effort to go out in style as I was. As we were sitting in the restaurant I said to her

—Yetta. Lets get a little bead serious.

**51**

—Whot is it? she was esking me.

—Well, waht do you think about me? Be honest to yourself and tell me.

—Well, I think you are a very nise gentleman.

—You think so, I said to her. Now I will ask you a few questions. I understand you are working in a tie facktory. How much money are you making in a week? Dont be bashwool.

—I am getting $9.00 a week.

—How do you getting along on that small salary?

—I mannaged . . .

In the meantime dooing the dinner we were densing and we enjoyet the hole evening. In the main time dooing the evening I ask her

—Where is your Family leaving? And how manny in your Family?

—I have a sister Rose, she replied, and two brothers, all leaving in Buffalo, N.Y. My sister Rose is maried. Very well off married to Abe Kushenbaum and they have a bussines, incondecent Light Co. My Father and Mother are also in Buffalo.

—What maid you to come to Chicago?

—Well, I will tell you. I have a Lady Frend from Yurop wich we all come from Walkewick, Russia. And she is very well off heer in Chicago maried and she invited me to visit with her here in Chicago. So my sister Rose gave me monney to go to Chicago for a while. Wen I came here and I lookt around I desidet to remain here. In the main time I find that job in a tie facktory and I like the city Chicago much more opertunity than in Buffalo. And here I am.

—Very ambishus, I said. Beautiful story. I like this. That mins I am the locky one to find you . . .

By that time got pretty late and I felt that she hat get up pretty early in the morning.

—Well, lets go home.

Took her home. Kised goodnite.

In the next couple of days I notised that she had not much close on her back. I went to Mandel Bros. Dep Store and bought her the entire outfit from had to tows. All kind off underwear, stockings, Blouses. And what-not. I remember exactly that I spent about $150.00 for her outfit. Two big boxes came to her from Mandel Bros. I want you to know that thus days $150.00 was lots of monney.

When she came home from work she find all of this in her room.

Well, dont ask.

When I came Wednesday to see her she says to me,

—Did you do that?

—Yess. I did.

—Why?

—Well, I will tell you later.

We went out again. I went in a secludet place so I can sit wit her alone. . . Then I stardet to explain to her my thinking and how much I think of her.

—Darling, lets not go around the burches. Just in plain words. I love you and want you to be my wife. Now give me your enser.

She was startled for a while and then she fell into my arms and stardet crying and said to me

—I exept.

The next day we went to Milwaukee Ave. and I bout her a cout, hat and gloves to match.

The fowloring Saterday we went out. We whore in a restaurant. I said to her

—Darling. I understand that you are making $9.00 a week selery.

—Yess.

—Now this is whote I wont you to do. I wont you to quit the job. Becouse $9.00 a week is very little. From now on I will pay you $9.00 a week and stay home until we get merried. I definitely insist you not to go to work.

—Can you afford this?

—If I couldn't I wouldnt deside to get married.

Thus days I was considert an establishet young men. I was making $50.00 a week and $50.00 a week was a lot of money. Not many young men was in my standard.

We finely set a date for our engagement. Of corse my Sister in low Hellen did not love to much me getting married, but this is it. In fact she tried to discourage me. Butt my Promised was maid and I will never brake a Promised. In fact the engagement party was made in my Brothers home. Lots of my Family, frends, came to the party. And we said a date for the wedding.

Yettas sister Rose maid the wedding in Buffalo. The date for the wedding was in March the 25, 1916. My Sweathard Yetta

*tears came to her beautiful ies*

went to Buffalo two weeks ahed of time to her sister to make preparation for the wedding. I came in 3 days befor the wedding. That was the first time that I med up with my sweadhards Family. The wedding took place in her sister Roses home. It was verry nise. There again the hole *Mishpoche* (that mins relatives) were invited. They treated me very nise.

Two days later I took the bride my wife and went back to Chicago. We rented a very nise appartement. Four rooms in a brand new building. The rental for apt was 12 months. We went over to a furniture store that my Unckil *Shuchmann* was meneger there and furnish aut the four rooms complete from soap to nuts. The intire cost for the 4 rooms amounted to $700.00 carpenting and all the furniture.

In fact it was a Dream.

She became a wanderful houskeeper. Her cooking and baking was out of this world. I useto work extra overtime to make more money to bring in the house. We made lots of frends, we had lots of company. Oll in oll we whore a happy couple. . . .

# ‹10›

## CHEPTER THAT ONE OF MY EMPLOYERS BROKE HIS PROMISED

Efter I got meried, I left the firm Agnion and Rubenstein and went to work in another Costume Jewelry factory. My nature was olways consianches—to work faitfull and trying to do best. Lanth of hours did not ment nothing to me. I olways tried to do the best on the job that I am hired that was· in me. Oll the time. I never was tieyard.

My bosses name was Mr Liler.

Ones that Mr Liler colls me in his office.

—Sami, I was watching you oll the time the way you are working and the way you carrying youself as a fine young men. Therefor I am going to make you forman of that shop. You runit and I promise you by the end of the year I will give you a $500.00 bonus.

I looked at him and I said

—Mr. Liler, is that a promise?

—Yessir. So help me god.

And with that I said

—O.K. I shell do my best.

And I wolked out from his office with the understanding that by end of the year I will resive a $500.00 bonus of wich that ment this days lots of money.

Well, I Sami worked very hard. I put in lots of overtime, working nites Saterdays and som time came don on Sunday to work. I put in time in one year olmost like two years of hard laybor. Mr Liler everytime he so me was smiling of the job I· was dooing.

In the maine time my wife was very happy that by the end of the year will get rich and having such wanderful Bonus. So we desidet to have a child and my wife begin in Pregnency. We wouldnt have to worry about any expencence, we will have enoff to pay for everything. Yes, everything is fine and we have been very happy oll the way true.

Finely the year came around and I sure thoght when

Christmas comes around I will get the $500.00 check.

Christmas came around. No check.

No money.

Well, I thoght, I supose he, Mr Liler will give befor New Years.

New Year came around. Againe no check.

No Money.

Finely I went to the office and Liler said to me

—Sami, you want to see me?

I said

—Yessir I do.

He understood that I came for the check that he promiced and he turns around with a engry voice.

—Mr Liler, I said, how about my check you promised?

—What check? I never promised you anything.

—No, you did not, I said. O.K. Very well. Good by, Mr Liler. I will see you in court.

—Get out!

I did. Went out and I came to see a frend of mine a lowyer. I told exsectly my story word by word and he says to me

—Have you a contract to this efect?

—No, I havent.

—O.K. Very well. Will get that money with oll the expence of the court and my fee too.

In the maine time the next day I went to work in another factory with more pay than I was getting from Mr Liler.

In the maine time I was coled to court wher the case appered. He Mr Liler came to court with two lowyers against me. The judge herd his side of the story. Then he coled me. I as a little young men told the judge my side of the story. By the end of my story I again stood up and I says to the judge

—Your Honor, may I tell you somting else?

—Yes, young men, you may.

Then I proside.

—You honor, on the stranght of Mr Liler promise to me that I will get $500.00 bonus end of the year I desidet to raise a family and I will not have enoff money to pay the expenses for my wifes pragnecy.

The Judge kind of smiled and the intire court became in

60

lefter. Finely the Judge said to me

—Young men, stand up in front of me. And look straid in my ies. You Mr Liler, you to stand up long side of this young men.

Then the Judge came out with a wordic.

—Pay this young men oll of it with oll the expence atecht to this case. Judgment note.

The case was finished. I got clear $500.00 to my self. A year later the same men apologiest for me and I have forgiven him for his conduct and we became frends again.

My Motor in life is to forgive.

Never carry a groudge on anybody that makes a mistake in his or her life.

**‹ || ›**

# CHEPTER OF MY FAMILY AND MY BUSSINES

We had our first child a boy. To our misfortune the child wasnt rite. Som how it was a retardet child. Couldnt talk or walk. It was no hopes and no doctor gives us any encorengment. When it was two years old the child died.

That was a offul shock to us. My wife was very hard sick about it.

But little by little she came to herself. And then two years later came my daughter Burnise, and then our son Lloyd. In Yidish was *BROCHELE* and *LABEL*. Then along came our son Howard, in Yidish *HECHELE*. And finely the last child in our family, Millie, Mildred, the *MIZINKE*. So it was al together four childrn. Two girls and two boys.

In the main time I am going on with my Desighning and Engraving Costume Jewelry. I was a forman in a Comb factory in the shop. One day I got a telephone coll from one of the large firms in Chicago. A wholesaler in the Costume Jewelry. The name of that firm was knowen as Morris Mann and Riely. The telephone coll was that I should come to see Mr. Morris. I was very flethered that such big company wanted to see me.

So I went in to their place of bussines. At that time they were located 105 So. Wells Street. I went in and I met up with Mr. Morris. He greeted me with warem Hand Shake.

—Sami, he said to me, How would you like to become one of us in our instution? I am taulking to you that you should

*Mr. Mann*

64

open up for us a Comb Dept. and who knows? Som day you may manege for us the intire Hair Ornament Dept.

Mr Morris was a very smart man and very convinsing. I so at that time a big potential for me.

—Mr Morris, I said, Whote is your offer as far as my salary is consern?

—Sami, I will stard you at $35.00 a week with advensment befor long.

I exsepted that offer.

I maid a Deal and I stardet to organize. The first thing Mr Morris send me to Leominster, Mass. to by material. At that time the maine bying for all the Costume Jewelry was in Leominster becaus that was the maine manufacturing city on Hair Ornaments. And Hair Ornaments was the fondation of the Costume Jewelry. At that time Providence, R.I. wasn't much knowing as a Costume Jewlry Center like to day. In Providence then they were making only solid gold little rings, small chain necklesses. They had only a few facktories.

I so the opertunity when I maid the Deal with Mr Morris that befor long I will menege the entire 2nd floor for Morris Mann and Reily. And so it was. My dream came trugh. Efter beeing with the firm one year I became the entire boss of the 2nd floor. Mr Morris stardet to send me to New York . . . Boston . . . Leominster, Mass. to style and buy material for that Dept.

*My dream came trugh...*

In Leominster Mass. by making Hair Ornaments and Spanish Combs, that was the attrection for Costume Jewelry. All of this was made out of Celelouid. It was cheap labor in Leominster. Italian and French pipple. Craftsmen.

Efter I was running the Hair Ornament Dept for two years, Mr Morris send me on the road. Selling Hair Ornaments. My selery was $40.00 a week, with $35.00 travelling expenses. Out of the $35.00 travel expences I useto save up $5-6.00 of the week and bring my wife and childrn a present when I came home.

# ‹12›

## ON THE ROAD FOR MORRIS MANN & REILY
## FIRST TREVELLING.

67

In the days from my first expirence treveling on the road my $35.00 a week for expences covered everything—buss fair, hotel, food. Very seldom I used a Porter, or a cab—unless it was epsolutlie nessarrie. I trevelled all nite and when I came to my destination I went to the Hotel Milner. In thus days reservations wasnt nesserie. You can olways get a room. The prise for the hotel was ¢75 a nite.

I useto carry over myself my personal belongings and my sample cases from the station and then carry up to the room. If it was to heavy to carry I useto live some belongings at the station and make two trips back and fort. I was never particular whot kind of room, just so it had klean bad and wash room. At times there wasnt even hot water.

I treveld all nite on the buss or on the train, slept the best I could. Winter time I coverd up with my overcout and felt pretty good. I came in the hotel in the morning. When I came to my room I shaved, wash myself with toren towel, just so it was clean. I changed my shirt, went down for brackfest, lited up my 2 for a nickle Cigar and was redy for bussines. By the way, my expence for the hole day—$2.00 a day, food and hotel. I olways menege to find a coffeteria to save the tipping to the waitress.

And heer is my Expence account:

¢ 15 cents Brackfest
" 25   "    Lunch
" 75   "    Dinner
" 75   "    Hotel
____
$1.90
.10 tip for Dinner to waitress
____
$2.00
.15 for Cigars for the day
____
$2.15

The Cigar was the only extravagin thing that I had in the early days. I shell give you illustration of the food we were getting. Namely, Brackfest. I had orange juice. One egg. Cofee. No tip. Cofeteria. ¢15.

Lunch. Again cofeteria. Soup—any kind. Sandwich and cofee. No tip. ¢25.

And som time I useto go in to saloon. Have a glass of beer for ¢5 and on a long table useto be oll kinds of delicatessen for Free. As long as you bought a glass of beer, on the long table was harring, hard boiled eggs, Salami, redishes, cheez, green onions and bread. Eat oll you want. For that kind of a fist you would pay $2.50 to day.

I useto stay in a city 2-3 days to coll on costimers. The murst you can make is 2 citys a week. The buss from Chicago to St. Louis cost $2.50. From St Louis to Kansas City $2.00. And back from Kansas City to Chicago Home $3.50. My intire expence for the week—

$ 8.00   Buss Fair round trip
$12.90   Hotel and Food
—————
$20.90

When I came home Saterday after the week, I saved up $10-12 that I useto give to my wife and the childrn from my expence account as a present. That was one of the mottors of my life of treveling—to save up from my treveling to bring as much as I can to my wife and childrn.

I shell never forget in my younger days of treveling the expirence we had to go true, the suffering we had. There were no air condition rooms. Espacialy in the south. 105-110 degrees, the heat. So at nite we useto put under the bad a cake of ise to cool up the room in order to be able to sleep for a couple hours. In the morning the floor was full of water. South, north—oll the same. The same Milner Hotel, the same cofeteria, the same food, olmost the same expence. But for

Sami everything was fine, just so there is a costimer of Costume Jewelry to coll on. Selling for me was no problem.

I loved to meet my costimers, espacialy when I had a Cigar in my mouth. I was like a tiger from the cage—but I never hurt anybody or insulted anybody. My mottor is to be Humbil to my felow men at all times. I olways kept cool, and polite regardless sale or no sale. I olways had a kind worth for annabody. I useto uproch my costimer olways with a smile. Of corse the Cigar in my mouth was olways a big help, whenever I felt down in the dumbs. The smoak useto tell me, Sami go forward. Straighten you self up. I will not let you down.

Costimers would not recognise me unlest I had a cigar. Even when a costimer did not smoak they olways liked me and my cigar—and for that reason for me beeing so humbil came the sucsess in my life. A multitude of frendship. No matter who he or she was—costimer, my colligs, sailesmen or just strenger—olways a kind warem grittings. A he or she. I never had a grim face. Olways with a smile.

*the smoke says "Sami, go forward"*

I havent been too edjacated. I had no edjacation of spelling or writhing. This reminds me one time I came in to a costimer. In the Costume Jewelry they useto by by colors. I was writing an order. That costimer asked me fuchia. I did not know how to spell it. I turned to the costimer and I said

—*Dog gun net,* you spell it.

Until to day werever he meets me that costimer reminds me that I was not able to spell that color. I can go on and on and tell you stories and insidents of my treveling with the Costume Jewlry in my life with aut a stop.

# ‹13›

## CHEPTER OF MY OWN BUSSINES

I was treveling for about 2-3 years for Morris Mann and Reily and finely I desidet to open up my own factory.

One morning I came back from a bying trip and I went in to Mr Morris office and I said

—Mr Morris, I am going to quit.

He was kind of startle.

—Why? he said in a kind of engry tone.

—Lets not get engry on one another, I said. I will explain you my reason for quiting you. Not for money. I am not looking for a raze. That was not the Qweshion in my mine.

—Then whote is your problem? Mr Morris said to me.

—I will tell you. I am going in bussines for myself and I will open a factory in my own name.

—Well, I admire your ambishion, Sami. How will you get credit to stard that factory?

By that time I lit up my cigar.

—Mr Morris, you will give it to me.

He stardet to leff a little bead.

—Mr Morris, dont leff it off. If you dont som other pipple will. But I come to you first and I promis you that I will not neglect your department, even when I move out. I will not leave you dry. I shell make in my factory that I will open up shortly, all the goods you need for your Hair Ornament Department. I shell charge the prises accordingly that would not cost you any more than on your own. You will safe space and paying money for help in the department. But I olso want you to understand that I will sell my product to other hole-salers in the Country. But no metter whot I'll do, I shell take care of you.

—Com over tomorrow and we will talket over, he said.

So we made an arengement that in my bussines merchandise for Mr Morris would come first befor anabody else. I stardet my bussines on my reputation. The manufactures in Leominster gave me credit on open account. But of cours I new that the first account of Morris Mann and Reily would give me the first stard, and would pay me every week of the merchandise that he would send to me.

And it worked out for both of us. I had a frendship then thru the years with Harry Morris. I had coffee at 9 A.M. in his office and consolt verayes thing about bussines with him. And manny times he was taken my advise at the end. I dont want to forget to mention that when Mr Morris past away, his lawyer coled me to com over and pick up a check for $1000.00 that Mr Morris left for me in his Will.

In the main time I rented the space for the facktory on North Avenue and Damen Street. Wile I rented this space I new that I needet somone to work and take care of the shop. By that time I thought of one man that workd at another Comb factory by the name of Sam Goldfarb.

I coled him up and said

—Sam, how would you like to become a partner to me?

He agreed. We maid up papers between us of wich he invested $3000.00. He quit his shop the same day and became a full partner wit me.

75

Imeadiately efter I had my space rented and my partner sighned I went to Leominster to by merchandise from veriyus facktorys that manufacture Hair Ornaments. I arenged the amount of credit from all kind of difrent factorys.

When I came home I stardet to orgenise my own factory. Merchandise stardet to come in and I stardet to make my sample line. I was a good desighner and a good sailesmen. That was my reason of taking in a partner for the shop so he can be the inside men of the factory and I will be the out side men of bying and styling and selling to the costimers.

The first costimer I coled was Mr Morris and maid a date to show him my sample line. He greeted me very nise and gave me a $5000.00 order. We maid arengment that he should pay me upon reseving the goods, as I needet money to running my bussines. I maid speashial prises so it would be interesting for him.

Then I stardet to see other jobbers. My partner Sam Goldfarb stardet to hire help for the shop. The work was consisting of engraving, drilling and setting stones in combs, barrettes and hair pins.

The name of the company I named it THE ART COMB ENGRAVING COMPANY.

Before long I got to be knowing as Sami with the cigar. Wit out my cigar I couldnt stard thinking and talking. . . . that was my Symbol.

# ‹14›

## PARTNERS IN MY BUSSINES

As I was conducting my bussines I notised ever time I went don-ton to see som costimers whenever I came back to my factory Sam Goldfarb my partner useto take out his watch and look at his watch. We are in bussines together alredy a year. He lookd at his watch when I came in.

That was going on for several weeks. Finely I got some suspishions. I thoght, Whote in the wold is he dooing? Is he looking and timming me how long and how much time I spend? I have a cup of cofee with a costimer, a launch with a costimer? Or maybe its only a hebit.

One day I came in and the same thing. So I said

—Sam, whote are you looking at the watch? Are you watching my time, how long I'm gone, whote I'm dooing?

He turned red in the face. One word lead to another. I dont like this. I'm the main man, I go to sell merchandise, for him as well as myself. I cant worry whote time I come beck.

—Sam, I said, Thats it. You cant be no more my partner. Lets divide right now. One way. Ither you pay me out, you remaine. Or I will pay you out. You can go back to the bench.

—No, he said. You pay me out. I will not be able to runnit by myself, that I know.

The next day I went with him to the bank and I maid arengment of wich the bank borought me som money. I paid him out. He was a nise man. But not smart.

In the main time I had a very good frend, the byer from Sears Roebuck. Sam Blumenthal. Sears Roebuck thus days had also a speashial faktory for combs. One day the byer from Sears coled me up and said

—Sam, I have a nise young men that works for us in the Comb Dept. How would you liked to have him for a partner to you?

I sure needit a responsible men in my faktory. This young

# New Barrette Creations

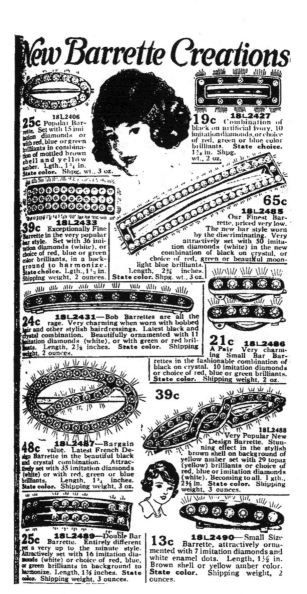

**25c** **18L2406** Popular Barrette. Set with 15 imitation diamonds or with red, blue or green brilliants in combination of mottled brown shell and yellow amber. Lgth., 1¾ in. State color. Shpg. wt., 3 oz.

**19c** **18L2427** Combination of black on artificial ivory, 10 imitation diamonds, or choice of red, green or blue color brilliants. State choice. 1⅛ in. Shpg. wt., 2 oz.

**39c** **18L2433** Exceptionally Fine Barrette in the very popular bar style. Set with 36 imitation diamonds (white), or choice of red, blue or green color brilliants, in a background to harmonize. State choice. Lgth., 1½ in. Shipping weight, 2 ounces.

**65c** **18L2485** Our Finest Barrette, priced very low. The new bar style worn by the discriminating. Very attractively set with 50 imitation diamonds (white) in the new combination of black on crystal, or choice of red, green or beautiful moonlight blue brilliants. Length, 2¾ inches. State color. Shpg. wt., 3 oz.

**24c** **18L2431**—Bob Barrettes are all the rage. Very charming when worn with bobbed hair and other stylish hairdressings. Latest black and crystal combination. Beautifully ornamented with 11 imitation diamonds (white), or with green or red brilliants. Length, 2⅜ inches. State color. Shipping weight, 2 ounces.

**21c** **18L2486** A Pair Very charming Small Bar Barrettes in the fashionable combination of black on crystal. 10 imitation diamonds or choice of red, blue or green brilliants. State color. Shipping weight, 2 oz.

**48c** **18L2487**—Bargain value. Latest French Design Barrette in the beautiful black and crystal combination. Attractively set with 35 imitation diamonds (white) or with red, green or blue brilliants. Length, 1¾ inches. State color. Shipping weight, 3 oz.

**39c** **18L2488** Very Popular New Design Barrette. Stunning effect in the stylish brown shell on background of yellow amber set with 29 topaz (yellow) brilliants or choice of red, blue or imitation diamonds (white). Becoming to all. 1 xth., 2½ in. State color. Shipping weight, 3 ounces.

**25c** **18L2489**—Double Bar Barrette. Entirely different yet a very up to the minute style. Attractively set with 16 imitation diamonds (white) or choice of red, blue, or green brilliants in background to harmonize. Length, 1¾ inches. State color. Shipping weight, 3 ounces.

**13c** **18L2490**—Small Size Barrette, attractively ornamented with 7 imitation diamonds and white enamel dots. Length, 1½ in. Brown shell or yellow amber color. State color. Shipping weight, 2 ounces.

men was working as a driller in the comb dept. at Sears setting stones.

—And beside, the byer said, if you will take him in, you have a chence to get bussines from Sears Roebuck. His name is Joe Plotkin and he comes from a very nise Family.

I made an agreement with Joe Plotkin to take him in as my new partner to my bussines. He was a very agresive young men and the byer from Sears turned over lots of bussines as promised. They sent orders for merchandise to make for them speashily.

Joe Plotkin was very good in the bussines. One day he said he had a Brother in low that he liked him very much and he was looking to inwest in a bussines. Would I take the Brother in low for a third partner?

—Sure, I said. Room for Everbody.

At that time we could olways use a little cash.

So the Brother in low from Joe Plotkin became a silent partner. Mr Siggle. He was a nise men and very clever. We entertaint him soshially with his family. Ones we had a dinner and we were all sitting at the table. I lookd don and my watch was missing.

—Hey, I said. Mine watch is gone.

Mr Siggle was at the table with me. He gave a little smile.

—You lost you watch? He said.

—Yes, I said. I had it on a wile ago.

Mr Siggle stardet leffing and he took the watch out from his pocket.

—Here is your watch, he said.

Everybody was leffing that he could take the watch and I dint even no it.

## the pick pocket partner

One day I was having lunch at Morrises Restaurant. Mr Siggle had been a silent partner in mine bussines for a couple of years. I met a Cosin from Joe Plotkin outside the Restaurant.

—Sami, he said to me, come in here. I want to tulk to you. We sat don at a table.

—Sami, he said, whote in the wold are you dooing? Whote in the wold are you taking in a picpoket he should be your partner?

I looked at him. A picpoket?

—Yes, he said. Mr Siggle, the Brother in low from Joe Plotkin, is running a picpoket scool don-ton.

His own Cosin is telling me this. I remembered the watch. It dint dawn on me. The next morning I told Joe Plotkin. He was very upset. Not *my* Cosin is telling me this. *His* Cosin.

His own Cosin. A scool. For pikpokets.

In thus days on a Friday pipple carried their monney on the street car in a little envelope they got paid in. And picpoket men picked their pokets.

I paid Mr Siggle out the next morning.

—Lets not have any aggravation, I said to him. Mine bussiness is clean.

So that was the end of Partner No. 3. Joe Plotkin was my partner for 7-8 years. Then his Brother took him into the Lether

81

Goods Bussines, an old bussines, 50-60 years old. Joe Plotkin was a nise men and a good partner.

So efter Joe Plotkin left I didnt have any more partners.

Set.
Pieces.
l Value Back
Set. Decorated
nds in set and
s. Brown shell
State color.
ide combs, 3½
t, 2¼ ounces.

—A Beautiful
et with 48 imi-
ite enamel dots
design. Brown
th, 4¾ inches.
ounces.

—Fine Quality
Prettily deco-
on diamonds
el dots. Brown
gth, 4 inches.
ounces.

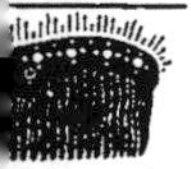

—Popular
et with 11 imi-
white enamel
s. Brown shell
State color.
ces.

—The New
an be worn in
rettily set with
s and white
4¾ inches.
amber color.
weight, 1¾ oz.

**48c**
**18L2469**—Popular
Style Ques-
nb. Very
gth, 4¼
tation dia-
mel dots.
Shipping

**$1.35**

**18L2414**—Stunning up to date style Pin in the fashionable demi-shell color (mottled brown shell and yellow amber). Becoming to all types. Artistically set with 60 imitation diamonds (white) or choice of red, green or beautiful moonlight blue brilliants. **State color.** Length, 5½ inches. Shipping weight, 4¼ ounces.

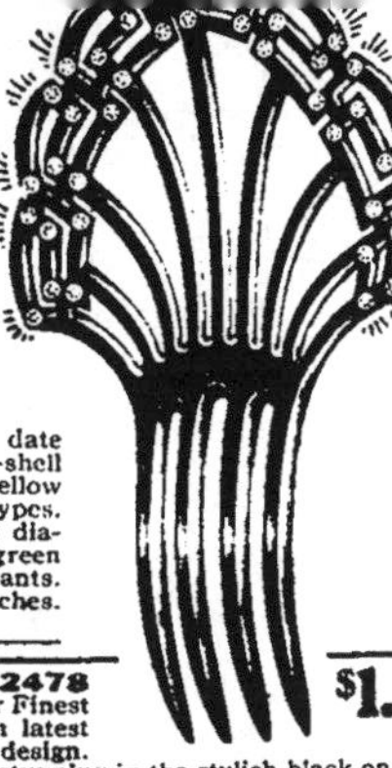

**18L2478**
Our Finest
Pin in latest
Paris design.
**$1.98**
Very stunning in the stylish black on crystal set with 42 imitation diamonds (white) or with red, green or the beautiful moonlight blue brilliants. Popular for evening wear. Unusual value. **State color.** Length, 6½ inches. Shipping weight, 6¼ ounces.

**$1.19**

**18L2479**—Very Popular Fan Shape Spanish Pin. Beautifully ornamented with hand engraved design. Attractively set with 16 imitation diamonds (white) or with red, green or blue brilliants in a mottled brown shell and yellow amber color. Very stylish and becoming. **State color.** Length, 4½ inches. Shipping weight, 4¼ oz.

**49c**

**18L2481**—Popular Style Spanish Pin. Very effective in hair. 27 imitation diamonds (white) set in a beautiful mottled brown shell and yellow amber. Can also be had with red or blue brilliants. Length, 4½ inches. **State color.** Shipping weight, 1¾ ounces.

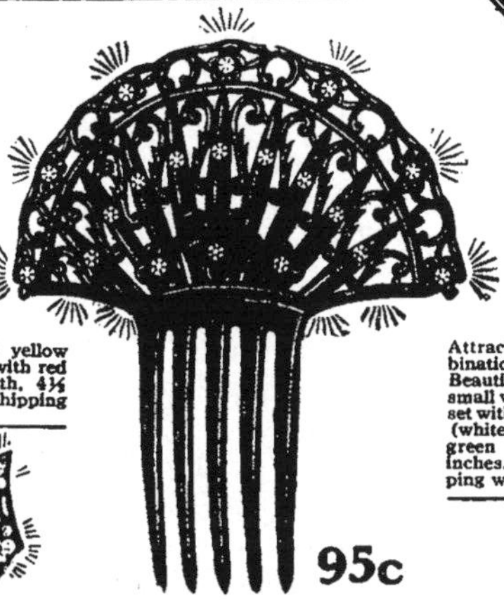

**95c**

**18L2484**—Popular large size Spanish Pin in beautiful open work design. Set with 19 imitation diamonds, in the fashionable mottled brown shell and yellow amber color. Sizes, 6¼x5¼ inches. Shipping weight, 4¾ ounces.

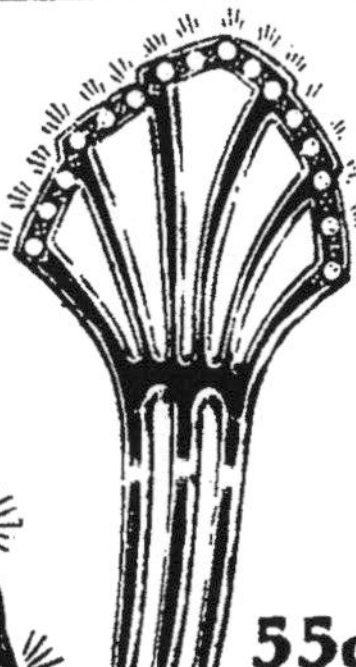

**55c**

**18L2483**—Exceptional bargain. Attractive Pin in the new combination of black on crystal. Beautifully ornamented with small white enamel design and set with 16 imitation diamonds (white) or with red, blue or green brilliants. Length, 5 inches. **State color.** Shipping weight, 4 ounces.

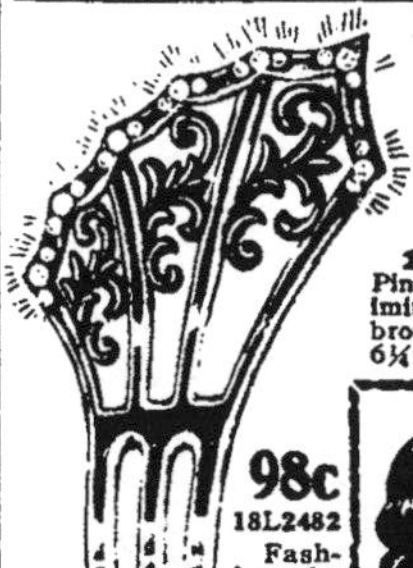

**98c**
**18L2482**
Fashion's Latest Filigree Design Pin. Set with 21 imitation diamonds (white) or with red, green or moonlight blue brilliants. Very attractive in the stylish demi-shell color (mottled brown shell and yellow amber). All the rage with new style hairdressings. Length, 6 inches. **State color.** Shipping weight, 4 ounces.

**Charming Head Band**
**79c**
**18L2405**
Most stylish for wear with bobbed and full style hairdressings. We offer this very popular style at a low price. Made in leaf pattern of brilliant metallic cloth in gold or silver. Length, 18 inches. **State color.** Shipping weight, 5¼ ounces.

**27c**

**18L2480**—Excellent Value Small Size Spanish Pin. Very attractive in the stylish demi-shell color (beautiful mottled brown shell and yellow amber) set with imitation diamonds or with red, green or the beautiful moonlight blue brilliants. Length, 4 inches. **State color.** Shipping weight, 1½ oz.

**67c** A Pair
**18L24**
are extra
Side Comb
imitation
pair, and decorate
enamel dots. Very
Length, 3¾ inches.
color only. Shippin

**19c** A Pair
**18L2400**
Quality Side C
wavy line top.
inches. Brow
low amber color.
Shipping weight, 2 ou

**38c** A Pair
**18L2494**
Good Quality
Neatly decorate
enamel dots and
diamonds in pair. Bro
only. Length, 4 inche
weight, 2 ounces.

## *Fine Tuck*

**45c** A Pair
**18L2826**
Popular Shape Hinged Braid Pins. Very effective in hair. Set with 22 imitation diamonds in pair and white enamel dots. Brown shell color only. Length, 2½ inches. Shipping weight, 1¼ ounces.

**18L2419**
Charming Crescent Shape Hinge Pin, set with 14 imitation diamonds, or choice of red, blue or green brilliants in background to harmonize. Can be worn singly or in pairs. Stylish demi-shell color. Length, 2¾ in. **State choice.** Shipping weight, 1¾ ounces.

**33**

**19c** A Pair

**18L2852**—T
diamonds and whit
are set in this p
Combs. Very po
value. Length, abo
Brown shell colo
weight, 1 ounce.

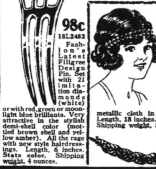

# *Bridal and Confirmation Wreaths*

**75c**
ation wreath, made
vers, branched with
dy high class work-
ecial value for this
or shipment, 7½ oz.

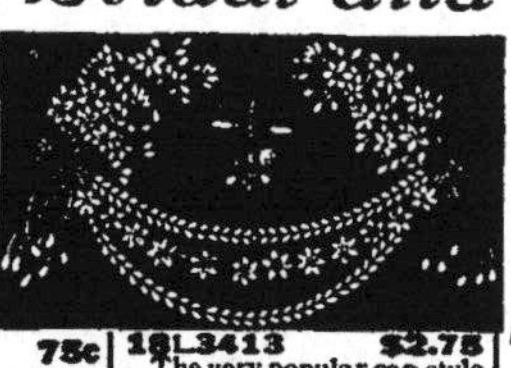

**18L3413** **$2.75**
The very popular cap style bridal wreath; very dainty and most becoming. Beautifully made of white wax in orange blossom, dainty buds and green leaves. We recommend this for its good style and fine qual-

**18L3411** **$2.25**
A fine looking bridal wreath, similar to 18L3413, but not quite so full. Splendid value. Shipping weight, 9 oz.

**18L3419**
**19c**
Bridal or confirmation bouquet. Beautiful wax flowers and buds with two green leaves.

**18L3415** **$2.69**
Our special full coronet style with long trailing ends. Carefully made of white wax in orange blossoms, buds and tiny green leaves.

**18L3417**
A fine bridal or
wreath in new sty
white wax in
buds, set off with

s Roebuck and Co.

# ‹/5›

## CHEPTER OF CARSON PIRIE SCOTT & CO.

In the 1930's I was at that time a very sucsesful Manufacture in the Costume Jewelry. I was manufacturing only Hair Ornaments. Everything out of Selelouid. That was the main idums in the Costume Jewelry Filld. Without a Hair Ornament you wasnt in Costume Jewelry. In fact at that time I was considerd one of the biggerst in the Field. I olways sold to the wholesaler. Never sold to the retail stores.

I olso was knowing oll over in the Industry as Sami with the cigar. With out my cigar wasnt me. When I had to make a sale or call on a costimer I useto lite up my cigar and the smoak from the cigar help me make dessision of my bussines and think how to sell and whoet to do.

At that time my factory was at 317 W. Monroe St. I had 10,000 sqware feet. Around the block from my factory was one of the largest wholesale houses in the country, Carson Pirie Scott and Co. Now Carson Pirie Scott has only a retail store, but in thus days they sold wholesale and so did Marshall Field. Marshall Field at that time had a big wholesale division right across the river on Adams Street.

Carson Pirie Wholesale. Oll the wholesalers knew Sami. Only I didnt have this costimer, right around the corner from my factory. I Sami maid up my mind to get some bussines. To get this costimer ment to get additional from 250 up to 300 thousand dolers a year.

The name of the byer from Carson Pirie Scott was Mr Lake.

The first time I came in his office I introdust myself. He kind of smiled but no date or given me the opertunity to bring in my samples. But for Sami there was no stop. I maid up my mine to come in to see him tweis a week.

—Good morning, Mr Lake.

Again with the same smile to me like anybody would.

Of corse efter a wile with me comming in tweis a week regular, he got to know me pretty good. I will never forget his exprestion on his face when he useto see me on his floor and he useto say to his assistant

—Here he is again, the forsable sailesmen. Dont he ever get tired?

That he dont know. Sami never gets tired.

So in a kidding way som times he would say to me

—Here comes the little Jewboy.

And again

—Well, Jewboy, how are you today?

So I thoght to myself, The more you call me Jewboy, the more you'll fall for it one of these days.

For a soled one year I was comming in his office tweis a week. And when the year came around I said to my self, Well Sami thats enoph.

By that time I got to know olmost everbody on the floor from the Costume Jewelry Dept. I stopped one of the boyes that worked in that Dept. I was waitting for him out side lunch time and he says to me

—Sam Silverman. Are you waitting for som one?

—No, I said. I am waitting for you.

—Whoet can I do for you?

—Lets go to lunch 1st.

—O.K.

I took him in restaurant. His name was Droory.

—Now I want you to do me a favor. Oll I wont you to let me know when Mr Lake is going to New York on a byeing trip and whote train he is taking and whote time. Olso whoet Hotel he is staying in New York.

—Fine. That I will let you know.

I paid for his lunch and a peckadge of cigarrettes.

Fine. I am starding to aparaite. I know one thing. When I'll meet Mr Lake on the traine that will be intirely difrent. I'll have a chence to get better enquinted. Not to tulk any kind of bussines but more on the frendly side. You talk in general verias things but you dont taulk any bussines.

Sure enoph, one morning Droory from that Dept. coles me, telling me that Mr Lake is leaving the next day for New York and stopping at the Pennsalvania Hotel. Thats all I needet.

—Thanks Pall.

The next day I pact up my bag and maid reservation on the same train and at the same hotel.

I got on the train. The Porter fixed up my copartment. I was resting up for about one hour. Well Sami, I said to my self, it is time to take a little wolk true the train to find my susspect.

Sure enoph. He is in the third car. I wolked up to him.

—Hello, Mr Lake.

—Well, forgod Sake! Whote a surprise! Wher are you going?
—Going to New York, I repleid.
—Whote a coinsident, he repleid. Sitdaren.
—I am not intruding you?
—No, no, just the oposite, he repleid.

We stard tulking of vereas things. It was kind of interesting. I was telling about my family and he did likewise.

—By the way, I ask him, where are you staying in New York?

—At the Statler Pensalvania.

—Whoet do you know! I olso am staying therre. In fact for manny years I am staying at the Statler, I repleid.

Whote a lei. Oll my life I have been staying at the Martinique on 32nd and Broadway. Well Sami I said to my self, So far it works.

In the main time it got around 6:30 in the evening. I said to Mr Lake

—How about dinner?

—Fine, he repleid. Yes, I am getting kind of hungry, Sami. He colls me Sami olredy.

Very well. We washt up and went in to the diening room for dinner.

We had an enjoyable dinner together. Lots of lefter, lots of storys. And sofa and soan. I can fill he is getting a little warmer. I ordered a few drinks and before long around 10 o'clock in the evening I bid him Good nite and paid the bill.

In the morning I see him again in the diening room—in fackt he held a sit open for me. So we had brackfest together and finely we arived in New York. We checkt in at the Hotel and I turned to him and I said

—Mr Lake, lets meet for dinner at you convenience.

—O.K. How about 7 p.m.?

—Fine, thats good.

Sure enoph, it came around 7 o'clock I ring his room.

—O.K. I am comming don.

We went to dinner. We had a wanderful time that evening. The fowloring day I arenged theatre tickets. Naturly I took care of everything. Paid oll around. By the end of the week we were unsapratable.

When the week was over we pardet like two brothers. He, the prospactive costimer, esk me when I am going home.

—Oh, I have to stay another couple days. I got lots of work to do.

The fackt was I had to stay in New York like you had to stay in Osh Kosh Wisconsin. I just wantit him to go home ahad of me. A metter efect, I had nothing to do at this time in New York.

We said Good bey to each other and he thankd me for such wanderful time he had beeing with me and I remained to go home the fowloring day.

When I got back home I didnt show up at his office. I felt that mine mishion is finished now. I have time.

Finely two weeks went past. I didnt see him or coll him.

He coled me.

—Where the hell is you line?

—Just tell me when you will like to see it, I said.

—Tomorrow morning.

So I broght in my samples and when I showed the line he coled over his assistend. And he placed a beautuful order.

Since that day I began to do a Fantastick bussines in a short time. I supplied my Hair Ornaments for the intire dept. of Carson Pirie Scott. My dream came trugh.

We became together so frendly that when PESACH came around, the Jewish Easter, we had Mr Lake and his family to the Sader. I maid him wear a scoll cap to respect my religion. And he was eating the gefilte fish like nobodys bussines.

In fact we did so much bussines for Carson Pirie Scott that one day I got a telephone coll that Mr Pirie the President from Carson Pirie Scott wants to see me, Sami. Mr Pirie so that Carson Pirie Scott is dooing a fantastick bussines with the ART COMB ENGRAVING CO. He askd Mr Lake

—How come? How is ART COMB ENGRAVING CO. so great?

Mr Lake askd Mr Pirie if he would like to meet this young men, by wich he ment me, Sami.

—O yes, Mr Pirie said. I sure would.

So a couple days later I wolked into Mr Piries office. The resepshionist took my card in and she comes out.

—Go in. Mr Pirie will see you.

Mr Pirie is in a nise office, not fency, filld with lotta books and papers on his desk. Kinda small. Mr Pirie was about 80 years then, a little stout men. Very poliet.

—Hello, Mr Pirie, I said.

—Come inn, he polietly. Sidaren.

—You coled for me?

—Yess, I sure did. Mr Silverman, I see that we are dooing very nise bussines. Beautiful. Tell me, whote are you dooing for our Dept?

Right ther and then I knew whote he wanted. He wanted I should tell him that my merchandise is better than from any other manufacturers. That I would never do. I should tell him my merchandise is better than others? No. That would not be the right enswer to knock your competiter.

I lit up my cigar to give me inspiration. I must enswer directly to the point but I must use my diplomacy.

—I will tell you, Mr Pirie, whoet I do for you, I said. I ship to you merchandise. In returned you are sending me checks.

Mr Pirie got up from his chair.

—Young men, he said, I was told that you are a little devil. I am pleased to meet you. Tank you for comming.

So I went on with my relaitshonship with Carson Pirie Scott. Wholesale. Thrugh my relaitshonship with them I had one interesting experince. A firm by the name John B. Farwell closed their doors don-ton. The last day when they closed their

Mr. Lake wears a scull cap.

doors I heppend to wolk in to see whotes going on.

Mr Lake and oll the byers were in there on the floor working. When Mr Lake so me he coled out

—Hey, Sami, you want to by empty cartons?

He pointed up high on shelfs there were boxes.

I can olways use boxes.

—How much? I said.

—$10.00.

So I payed and they gave me resept. I forgot oll about it.

A couple weeks later here comes in my factory two big men and a truck. They say to me

—You got any help?

—What for? I said.

—We got for you a delivery from Carson Pirie Scott. But we

need help with it.

So I send my boys from the factory.

—Go don.

It was the boxes from John B. Farwell. They are bringing up boxes after boxes. I couldnt believe it how many boxes. Boxes upon boxes.

They were kinney heavy. We opend them up, we fond cases candelsticks, silverware, shoe polish, sope, trays all kinds, and hooks and Ies. The whole floor was filld with it. 12 thousand gross of hooks and Ies.

The byers from Carsons dint even look at it, up on the shelfs. They only cared whote was don on the floor.

I sold off the candlesticks, sope, shoe polish, silverware for $5000.00.

Then I still got left the hooks and Ies. One thousand grade gross, that is 12 thousand gross. Hoo can use that? I desidet farmers. On the farms they closed up thair aprons with hooks and Ies. So I went to a jober in Kansas City who sold to farmers.

—I got 1000 grade gross of this goods.

—How you came to get this? He asked me.

—I had a costimer of mine who went broke. I took merchandise.

He boght it. ¢25 a gross. Three thousand dolers.

So selling to Carson Pirie Scott and Co. was the end of my accomplisment as a little sailesman with a cigar.

# ‹16›

## A CHEPTER ABOUT MY WIFE AND CHILDRN

In the maine time wile I was working making a leaving for my family, my childrn were growing up.

Our first child Burnise (*BROCHELE*) was a very understandable child and good behaved. A little angil full of sunshine. She never made demends. She was good in scool, good at home. The Mother gave her Elocution lessons and she lernt pretty good. The Mother wanted to make a Ectrice from her and she was olways in Risitels. In fact when she became about 12 years of age she stardet to teach Elocution lessence to the naberhood childrn. And she was getting paid ¢15 a lessonce. Efter hy scool she was getting paid more and she was making 8-10 dollars a week. Later she became on the radio. She had a part in *The Romance of Helen Trent*.

Our next child Lloyd (*LABELE*) was olso very kind. Not such a good student in scool. He maid it, finished hi scool. But he was a willing worker. He olso understood his perents, and gave them love and respect. He useto sell papers in his spare time. He got a job at the Tribune to load papers on the truck at nite. Then he got a push card and sold ise crean around the house. From the ise crean he got a job in a grossery around the house on Lawrence Ave. The boss from the grossery liked him so well that he became the hole meneger. The boss paid him $12.00 a week and oll the grossery somtime for nothing to take home.

I will never forget one time Lloyd broght in 3 bags with grosserys to the house. The Mother askt

—Labale, the boss knows about this?

—He gave it himself.

Yet as a Mother she wanted to be sure. She went over to the grossery and she askt the boss

—My Labele broght in some food last nite. I would liked to know if you know about this.

The boss stardet to smile.

—Mrs. Silverman, a boy like Label, you dont have to worry

about him. I pact upmyself him the grosseries. Use it and eat it in good helth.

Label olways manegt to have money. He useto borough money to the kids in the naberhood. He olways had a dollar in his pocket. They useto pay him with interest. He never lost a penny from his costimers. They whore afraid for him. He was kinney husky.

Howard (Mother useto call him *HEVELE*) was a little on the wickling side, very quiet and polite. Good nature and good lissener. He never rased his voice above his wisper. He olways fowlored efter his brother Label. Label was his protector. Behind his back he useto be Lloyds helper. He helpt him sell papers. He helpt him sell ise crean. When Lloyd went upstares to eat lunch Howard stayd and watchd his ise crean stand. When a costimer wanted to by ise crean he never had the inishitive to sell him self. He stardet to holer

—Woide! Com don! A costimer!

As far as Howards scooling, he was excelent good student. He never gave us truble. Mother was olways watching him that he should not work too hard. She olso was Howards protector. Howard carried him self as a respectful gentelman and gave his perents love and respect.

Now comes my fourth child Millie (*LAYE*). She was difrent from any of my other 3 childrn. Mother favored her than anybody else wile she was a child. She had voice for singing. In Mothers ies she was a second Calucurchie. She stardet singing for nabors. Oll kind of songs. In the naberhood they useto trow pennys and nickels to her. We lived then in Albany Park.

The Mother stardet to praise her for everybody. Even stardet to bring her in the Sinagog to sing if ther was some entertainment dooing. She pracktist oll of the songs with out a ticher. To much money to give her singing lessence we didnt have but in Mothers ies she was a jéniust. Murst of the lessence

97

"Millie - THE MUUNK

she got was in scool. The singing ticher from the scool told the Mother that defently she, Mildred, will becom a star. Well, thats oll Mother had to heard. In other words she Millie got spoiled from so much praizing her. In the years to come she became very selfish. No advise from anabody. If Millie deside to do something nothing would help. She even lost respect for her perents.

Even her company of her girl frends Mother didnt liked. No metter whote Mother suggested Millie did the oposite. Millie was in a way beautiful. And consist som telent in her, but she did not use it in the right direction. Her aim is to be a leader but never finish anything. In later years she was singing in Sout Haven. She got a job for the intire summer entertaining gests at the Mishigan Beach Resort. She was kind and good to strengers, taking advise from strengers but not from her perents . . .

# ‹17›

## CHEPTER OF MY WIFE

Of course by me beeing on the road and not beeing at home didnt do too much good. My dear wife had to be the leader at home with oll the childrn and by her beeing alone and had to menege the hole family by herself that became very hard on her. When I came home on week ends she useto relait to mee oll the things that hepend dooing the week. I tried to comfort her the best of my nowlidge and to the best I know how and to explaine to her to take it easy and to take care of her own healt. But nothing would help.

In this case my dear wife was a little bead too strong minded and I had to be the Jodge and make the best desision for oll consurn. I personal my self never believed in spenking or howloring to the childrn. I just looked at each one and each went to there respected corner.

In fact I dont belive that spenking childrn is the remedy. I just taulked to the childrn in kind words and I find better results. My advise to all Perents—do not Howler. DO NOT SCOLD THEM in a meen way. Taulk to childrn with kindnes and love. You will be the Gainer. Childrn resent howloring and scolding. The same goes in Married life. He or she—act the same way. Your life will be much sweeter. It will be much more lovible for all consurn. Oll in oll if you take my advise your life at home will be a happy home.

In the main time out side of our problems raising childrn, making a leaving to provide for my dear family, my wife may she rest in pies, manegt her home in the morst wanderful menner that to my estimation ther was no one like her. Out side of beeing a good lovebile wife and good Mother to the childrn she was a wanderful hostage, olways having company, cooking and backing. She loved company. Her home was olways bright and shine. It was never a doll moment in her home.

She belongt to several organizations and to the sisterhood and sinagog and people hoo ever new her cared for her with the finest respect. She exsept everybody with open arms. Family and frends. She never let out a poor men with out given him donation or food as long as he reng her bell. She olways ask the poor men

—Are you hungry?

Give him food and maid him comfortable. Her cooking and backing was out of this world. At her home was olways Frailach and Lebedick. No metter how manny people in the naberhood came up she maid room for everybody. In the evening she loved to play cards. Pocker espeshol. The naibors olways had a game going. Aspecialy a few that she really liked —the Raymers, the Cohens, the Goldbecks, the Brooks, the Cavins, Mrs Miller and Sonia Marks. They oll lived on Kimball Ave in the 3600 block in Albany Park. Thes whore her favord.

Aspecily Friday nite by Mrs Silverman was a ball. People useto come for dinner to have a peas of gefilte fish and Yettas home baked challe and her own baked coffee cake. Even in the middel of the week frends would com over to eat and play cards until about 1-2 o'clock at nite. She was never alone when I was on the road. That was my wifes terepie and she endjoet. As long as ther was light in Yettas home they reng the bell with out any invitation.

In one way I was very happy that she was bizy and had company as I was olways treveling being morst of the time on the road. I felt that my dear wife has company and not longsom. In our life at home ther was love and infaction for one and other. My wife respected me as a husband and a men and I respected her as a wife and a good Mother to the childrn.

My wifes Mother, my Mother in low lived with us morst of the time. Her name was Etell. Wen she was not with us she livd with her douter Rose in Buffalo, N.Y. She was the morst love-bile old lady that I ever met. She olso was kind. Good. I have given her the hiyest respect as a lady and as a Mother. I olways tried to make her feel goot and have a goot home with us. My childrn olso have given her the hiyest respect as a fine Grand-mother. Espacialy my Labele and Brochele. They useto take her to sinagog and sit with her to the finish praying on Friday nite and Shabos morning. One of them went with her and than bring her home so she should not walk alone.

Raine or shine Labele the grandson was olways been neer his Grandmother, taking her and bringing her safe home from the sinagoge. He Labele olways fond the time for his Grand-mother. She useto bake cookies and bring it to the sinagog for the Onneg Shabat at the shul.

I olso recol the incident befor me leaving for the road. I olways meneged to leave on Sunday nite and oll the childrn useto get together to say good biy to me. Ther little ies fool with teers . . . ther daddy is going away for about 3-4 weeks. I useto give each and every one of them som spanding money, even if it was a nikel. Including my Mother in low. She useto put out her hand to get som spanding money. I shell never for-get her smile on her face. The Grandmother used to dahvn oll the time.

She died in our hom.

102

Oll in oll even tho we had som hard times we had good times in our hom and we whore one happy family to gether.

# ‹18›

## THE FIRE

One day in the morning I went donton esusual on bussines. About 12 noon I came back to my factory. When I got off the street car I notised on the corner my wife may she rest in pees, she was walking up and don on the corner waiting for me. When I so her, I said

—Honney, whoet are you dooing heer?

She said to me

—Lets go in the drug store to have something.

She wanted to comford me of the tregude of wich it confront me of whote heppend. So we went in the drug store to sit don at the counter. Then she turns to me.

—Honney, dont get frightend. There was a fire in the shop . . .

I fainted right there, and fell on the floor of the drug store. Because I new the nature of my merchandise—all Celelouid. It flames rite up in big flames when it burns.

Efter she rewived me, I went over to my factory.

There I find complete disester. They had to took half a dozen people to the hospital. My own partner Joe Plotkin got hurt also. The next thing I find out how that heppend.

One of the boys held a Spanish Comb in his hand. He was setting in some rhinstones in the comb and he tuched it to a hot electric plate. Just a tuch, and it flares up. He got scared and from exsitement he threw the flaming comb away from him and it landet on som stock and it all went up and stardet a big fire.

In the next couple of days I have rented a floor on Milwaukee Avenue and Damen. The byer from Sears Roebuck send in Mashines and stock and in less than a week we resume to aparate esusul.

I shell never forget when the adjusters from the Insurance Co. stardet to question me regarding my insurance.

—Mr Silverman, one of the adjusters ask me, you have

insured to much according to your inventory. You have to much coverage—your inventory showes only 5000 dollers and your insurance you took out is 25,000 dollers. How come?

Again Sami took out a cigar and I lit up. Thats the only way I can begin clear thanking.

—Yessir, gentlemen, you are right. I had only 5000 dollers merchandise. But the rest of my stock consist of my Desighns and Sketches. This are the rest of my stock. You deliver me my Desighns and Sketches and I will be satisfied with coveredge of 5000 dollers.

The adjusters looked on one in other and I Sami won the case. The Insurance Co. deliverd my ful claim on the insurance.

I fainted right there.

# -19-

## CHEPTER OF TAKING MY FAMILY TO FOX LAKE FOR THE SUMMER

This hepend in a time that my bussines wasnt very good. I hardly could make a leaving for my Family. In fact, I was very poor. About the 1st of June, when scool stoped, I was thanking to my self whoet I shell do with mine famile dooing the Summer.

Well, oll of a sutten it came to me an idia to rent a cotedge for the Summer in Fox Lake.

Sure enoph.

I did rented a cotedge for $75.00 for the intire Summer. Thus days $75.00 was a fency prise. I pact up my family and plased them for the intire Summer.

It wasnt bad. They had a place for swimming and having lots of fun. My wife was olso pleasd with the place. As for my self it gave me a briding spel. I was able to trevel and was trying to make a dollar altho the time of selling was very hard. Naturley every Saterday and Sonday I useto com out and be with my family. Sonday nite I went back home. I left my wife som money for the fowloring week. I needit a chence to think how to improve and whot to do.

Finely the Summer came to an end and I've got to bring my family back home. But one thing was on my mind—that I have got to pay the $75.00 to the lady that rented the cottedge. And beside the childrn got to go back to scool. They needit dresses and cloase, shoues and other things that childrn need olso, shirts, pants. Whot am I to do?

I thout I shell go over to my Brother Louie. Perhaps he can advise me whot to do. I went to my Brothers Wherhouse. He had a wearhouse of all kine of merchandise. When factories should go out of bussines, my Brother Louie would buy from them the merchandise. And sell it to pedlers. That was the Silverman Jobbing Co. on 18th St near Cermak Rd.

I told him my storey for him to advise me whote to do. He lisend to my sad story. Then he said to me

—How much money would you need to clear everything up?
He was so kind and good. I told him. Then I said
—How can you help me?
—Well, lessen, Brother. I tell you whot to do. You are a sailesman. Go and buy a cheap car and I will give you enoff merchandise in the car and you will probably sell it in the smoll country town. And you will have enoff to take care of oll your needs and you will pay me when you can.

So I went over to a garage from automobils in my naiberhood on Lawrence Ave and I said to the boss
—I need a car. But thats oll I have to spend is $25.00.
He pickt out an old jelapy, a big Nesh car.
—Young men, he said, heer is the car that will take you even to California.

I didnt have a drivers lisense but I boght the car and I coled up my Brother Louie and told him I had the car.
—O.K., he said, now com over.

So I drove over to my Brothers wearhouse and Sure Enoff, he pact me in stationery, scool books, pencil sets, rulers and toys. The car was pact to the top and heer I go to Fox Lake to bring my family home, with a fool truck of merchandise.

The car did not have any lisense, no City Stick, no nothing. I just boght it cut and dryed. Only God was with me that no polismen stoped me on the road. Aside from I dint have a drivers lisense. Fifty years ago who knew oll this monkey bussines with lisenses?

Anaway with oll the merchandise I pooled into Fox Lake about 7 P.M. that nite. My wife and childrn gave me a warem reception. Little that they knew that I have no money for the lady to pay for the cottedge. Oll I had with me was ¢75 in my pocket and a car with merchandise.

As usual my wife set the table for me to eat with the children. Efter dinner I said to my wife

*fifty years ago who knew all this monkey business with licenses?*

—Honney, lets put the childrn to sleep as we got to go in the city to see a costimer.

The childrn got washed up and they oll went to bad.

By that time was olredy 9 P.M.

—Whot costimer? my wife esked.

—Dont worry, I said. Just come with me.

So she got drest and heer we go.

I parked the car in the front from a drug store on the corner of the town sqware. I new this drug store carried oll the merchandise I had in the car. We went in to the store. It was olmost redy to close. We sidaren by the Ise Crean Counter.

As the boss from the drug store uproched us asking whot we would like to have I with a big smile said

—Two chocklet sodeys.

A sodey thus days cost ¢15. Thats ¢30 and I still got ¢45 left. So I boght a couple cigars. Without the cigar I couldnt use the pholosophy of the super sailesmen.

As we finish the sodeys was getting kinney late. I stardet tulking to the drug store men very conversational, about bussines and we became very chummie in a very short time. In mine own mine I figerd out that half the battle is over. Now I stardet to use my diplomicy and I said to him

—Say, lessen, I have lots of scool supplies in my car. Scool is starding next week. If you can use it the prise will be right. In fact you will make lots of money of the prise I will give you.

—What you got? he said.

—If youll permit me, I said and I godup.

—Go and bring in your merchandise.

I did and laid out on the floor every idum seprate. Pencils. Books. The prise I told him. I dint even no whote it was worth. But he said

—I tacket.

Then I said

—I have some beautuful toys. You can use som toys, dont you?

—Oh, you got toys?

—Sure.

Again he said

—Bring in.

I did. I empty out the entire car and the prise for the toys was olso exsepted. I sold him the entire merchandise of wich it came to $800.00 I want you to know that thus days $800.00 was a lot of money.

Efter he paid me cash right away, he was so heppy that he gave us for nothing two more chocklit sodeys. He said to me that he will coll me if he needs more scool supplys.

On the way back I said to my wife

—Honey, there is a God. I came to you with ¢75 and now I got $800.00 in my pocket.

The next morning I paid the $75.00 to the lady of the cottedge. We pact up our belongings and on the way home again I was thanking that I was driving with no lisenses and City Sticker.

Thank God. We came home, my wife got bizy to preper the childrn to scool. I paid my Brother for the merchandise. The prise he gave me was a little nothing—$150.00. So we had plenty money left to take care of our needs and I, the Super Sailesmen, took off for the road to resume mine bussines as usual.

The Nesh I kept for quiet awile. Finely I sold it for $50.00.

# ‹20›

## CHEPTER OF MAKING TREVELING DESSISIONS

In my treveling expirence with my Costume Jewlry I Sami never new exsectly when I am leaving for the road. Comming in the office in the morning that was the time I useto make up my miend when I am to leave. My wife or my childrn never know my tieming when I am to leave for the road. I was the mester, nobody had to tell me where to go and esfar the city, dint make any difrence. East. West. North or South. As a sailesmen I could sell America in any city.

Well, this is it. One morning I came to the office. As I finisht up with the morning mail I desidet to go the very same day to Cinncinnati Ohio. I coled my wife on the phone she should pack up mine bag, couple of shirts, my shaving and som other incidental things for me to take along.

—Where are you going, my dear?

—Yes, I desidet to go to Cinncinnati tonite.

—O.K. I shell bring everything you need.

In the maintime I pact up my sample cases. Redy to go.

I said goodbye to my wife and I went to the Union Station. I came up to the cage where they sell the tickets.

—Yessir?

—Let me have a ticket to Cinsinnati and a rummet.

I wanted to rest up dooing the nite and be fresh in the morning. The agent went back to look up a rummet for me. He comes back, opens up the little window and said

—Mister, I am sorry. All rummets are sold out.

By that time I litt up my cigar. With Sami with out a cigar no thanking.

—Is dat so, no rummet. Well, see whote you have in a rummet for St Louis.

Again he comes back with the sad story.

—Sorry. You out of luck again.

—Oh. By the way, Mister . . . I said. I stood for five minutes thanking. He wolked away. I smoaked my cigar. I had to coll him

—Com heer, Mr Agent. Whoet have you for Minneapolis?

He got oll exsidet. He opens the little window and linds turds me and said

—Mister, are you drunk? Do you know wher you want to go?

I turned rite back to him. I said

—Mister Agent, no wonder you are standing behind the cage selling tickets and standing in one place. Oll you know is to sell tickets behind that wholl. But I am a sailesmen and I can sell anewhers I go. It doesnt make no difrence to me. Any city— any part of the Country I have costimers and sell oll over the world. This is the difrent beetwin us. I am a Sailesmen and you will remain here selling tickets.

And the finale. I went to Minneapolis in a rummet and I sold ther just as well as in Cincinnati.

# -21-

## CHEPTER OF A COSTIMER 50 MILES FROM DALLAS TEXAS

Fifty years ago I had a little sideline. Selling dress trimmings. One interesting thing was the wife of the goverment from Kansas City. She had a hebit to make aprons. She maid beautuful aprons to give to her guests some gifts wenever she came or they came. They said to her

—Lessen. Wy dont you open up a factory? With your ideas you can do a wanderful job.

So she did. When I came to see her she had 500 people working for her in her factory and she used a lot of trimmings on her aprons. I sold her a line of buttons and fancy stuff. She took a liking to me and no metter whoet I showd her she boght. I lost track now of whoet heppend to her. She was the wife of the government of Kansas City. A beautuful woomen.

This reminds me of colling on this costimer fifty miles from Dallas Texas with my dress trimmings. At that time Dallas Texas had a lot of dress factorys. I had costume jewelry maid special for the dress manufactures—buttons, bukles. I heard about this factory when I got true with the city of Dallas. It was a big factory wich employed 1500 people. It was in Nacodeshes Texas.

So I desidet to get there. I never maid phone colls. It is very easy to say No on the phone. If you come without anything first it is a difrent story. Thus days there were no trains there only a bus. So I took the bus at nite. It seemd like I rode oll nite the fifty miles to get there. Neadles to tell you how hard and tiersome to get to that little town. Finely I maid it. The bus puled in about 7 in the morning.

I went in a barber shop and shaved. I put on a clean shirt and cleaned up. I had my brackfest until about 9 A.M. Well, it is time to go to my prospactive costimer. This is the first time that I shell try to do bussines with this factory.

I came in the front office. The resepshonist ask Hoo do I liked to see. I told her that I woold liked to see the boss or the byer.

—Yessir. Have you got a card?

—*Yesmem.*

—I presented her with my card wich she took. And I waited. It didn't took less then a couple minutes she comes out.

—Sorry. He is not interested at this time.

Well. Heer I treveld oll nite and no sale. I stardet to go out. As I was wolking to the dore, oll of a sutten I became a regular Perry Mason. I suttenly turned rite back to the younglady.

—Younglady, I said, I have given you my card. Woold you pleas be good enoph to go in your bosses office and get me my card back? Efter oll, this is my propirty.

She was startle for a minute, as she knew that her boss turr up the card and trowed it away in the waist besket. She turned red in her face. Then she went in her bosses office and I heard loud tulking. She told him that krazie lunetic the sailesmen wanted his card back. He olso must be startle since he knew dorn well he turr it up.

She came out and said to me that he will like to see me.

I knew then that he was a cook goose.

I went in his office with my sample case and he said to me ironicly

—Open up. Lets see whoets so importend for me to see.

—Nothing so importend, I said. But show me the courtesy to see my merchandise when I come oll the way heer to show it to you.

I opend up my case. When I got thru showing my sample line he gave me a $1500 order. And he thankt me for comming. I thankt him for the order and I went back to Dallas with accomplishment that I opend a new account.

*wife of the government of Kansas City*

# -22-

## MY BROCHELE GOES TO THE PROM

It was the time when Burnice my elder daughter was about to finich hy scool and esusual girls in scool stard tulking about thair prom. Hoo with hoom she should go to the prom with. Naturally being an aut standing girl in class—and olso being the mayor in the class—every one of the boys stardet to propose to her to take her to the Prom. But my Burnice had an Iie on one boy from the class. His nick name was Dummy Had. He was kind of leetle beet shei and was som how efraid to ask her for the Prom. And Brochele useto come home and consolted with Mother about the boyes. The Mother was olways her adviser and being as a sweet child and olso kind she olways lisendt to Mother and whotever Mother said thats it. She respected her Mothers dessission olways. Finely the boy Dummy Had askd Burnice for the Prom.

Well. Dont ask.

He was the President from the class, and even tho his nick name was Dummy Had I want you to know that he turned out to be a multimillionaire.

Even tho nobody knew that then, som how oll the girls was jellouse and oll the boyes was jellouse that Burnice is going to the Prom with Dummy Had. The Mother was so heppy that her daughter is going to the Prom with the finest boy in scool.

I will never forget that nite. The Joye and Frailachket it was in the house. Now comes the sad part.

I am to leave on the road by end of the week and I notised that my wife is kind of sad. I ask the Mother

—Why are you so sad?

The Mother linds over to me and said

—Brochele has no dress for the Prom.

And in reality there was no money for a new dress for the Prom. Bussines at that time wasnt so good.

I in torn esk how much time is to the Prom.

—One month.

—Well, dont worry, I repleid. For my daughter Brochele a dress for the Prom I'll get by hook and krook.

The fowloring day I went on the road for Detroit. In Detroit I had a very good frend. A dress manufacture. He was manufacturing party dresses. His name was Sam Sonenshine. His wife Sonia was there olso, the desighner in the factory. Lovely people. I came to them and I told them my story.

—My daughter Brochele is going to the Prom next month and I need a dress for her.

So Sam says

—Well, dont worry. I am going to fix up the finest dress that she will be the prettiest girl at the Prom.

And Sonia askt me her mesurements wich I described. She went in the sample room and we pict out a beautuful dress. White lace wich she went to fix up spacial for Burnice.

I said to Sam

—Sam, I have no money to pay you for the dress.

He turns to me and says

—Did I ask you money? You will pay me when you can. Whatever the material and labor cost that will cost you.

—O.K.

So I went on my visits, and the fowloring day when I was going home I went there and they had the dress ready. They packt it up in a pretty box and I got the dress for Burnise. Friday noon I left for home.

This was in winter time, January, and bitter cold but thanks god I maid it. The intire trip on the buss I was holding the dress under my arm thanking of not loosing the box.

Well, dont ask when I finely richt to my home and rang the bell. Oll the childrn stardet howloring

—Dady, Dady is comming.

Well, when they notised the big white box

—Whote is this?

Again they stardet howloring

—A dress. A dress for Burnise.

Well, I will never forget when they opend up the box and the face on Brochele and the Mother when they took a look on this dress. And olso my Mother in low was standing near my wife, oll of them together. As old as she was she was olmost densing from pleasure.

And Burnice rite away coled up the girl frends. There were two I remember Frida and Shirley Robinowitz. They whore unsepratable together oll the time. They came too, to admire the beautuful dress.

**128**

When the day came for the Prom we whore oll waiting until Brochele got drest, the intire family. Heer Dummy Had rang the bell and came upsters with a white corsage. The Mother did not slept the hole nite from Joy until Burnice came home in the morning to tell her everything that was going on the intire evening.

In a couple of months I paid them twenty five dollars for the dress.

# ‹23›

## CHEPTER OF MY EXPIRENCE WITH THE PEDLER TRADE

In my young days I represented manufactures off oll kind of boxed jewelry. Sets, such as pearl necklis, beads, braiselet and earring to match. As a set. This type of merchandise I was selling to the pedler trade. This was jobbers who useto sell to pedlers. Pedlers was push card kind of sellers, door to door. Like Maxwell St., some on Roosewealth Rd. I did a fantastic job with this kind of costimers oll over.

The murst of these costimers that sold to pedlers was at St. Louis, Cleveland, Detroit and Chicago. They had little stores. Ther was never room enoph to display my samples of the box goods. Ther was no sample room. In many cases I useto display oll of my samples on the floor. I had to open up my sample case outside of the store as you can hardly go inside. Sometimes I had to show my samples on the street altogether to thos men.

This type of people at times they whore very ruff, not humbil to the sailesmen. To top if off som of them whore not intelegent. Olso in murst cases I have never given them a copy of the order. They didnt want it. If you give it to them they trow it away. They said Gimme a gross of this, a gross of that. And they wolked away from you. Very uprobt and rude. I useto mark don on a pees of paper the amount of quantity and that is the way this type of costimers was bying merchandise.

I personalie have down a very good bussines with them. I stodiet the charecters and esusual in turn I was very humbil. In fact the ruffer they whore the better I liked it. In a long time they became frendly to me. No more ruff stuff. When ever I came in they have given nice reseption. Sort of a welcome.

Ones I came in Detroit just to see my pedler jobbers. There were at that time about six pedler jobers in Detroit that I so on a regeler basis. But that time nobody of my pedler trade that I useto do such fabulas bussines did not want me at that time to give me any orders. They oll said they had enof goods and they

132

didnt needit.

I couldnt stand it.

I came oll the way to Detroit to see them. And by that time I new they should be out of merchandise and not one woold give me an order.

I went back to my hotel that nite. I had dinner and a good drink and I said to myself It cant be. I couldnt stand it. So I

became the byer for my pedler jobber costimers. I opend up my sample case and I stardet to give each costimer according. The smaler jobbers 600-700. The middle men jober 1000-1500. The big jober 2000-2500. You see I new I never give them a copy of the order and they havent got a copy because they didnt want it.

I maid up oll the orders and I send it in to my factory. I Sami prayed for about a month that it shoold stick. And you know whote? It did stick. They resived the goods and they sold it and they paid my factory on time.

So I didnt have to make a trip oll the way to Detroit for nothing.

# >24<

## THIS CHEPTER LESSON TO YOU, MR. SAILESMEN

To become sucsesful a sailesmen dont need to be a colidge gradjuate or a colidge men or even poor in gremer. To become a sucsesful men in selling first you must have common cents. You must be humbil, gentil and clean cut.

At first you must studie your product you are selling and you must know everything whats oll about it. You defently must know the product. When a costimer is esking you a question about your product, you must give the rite enswer. How it is maid and whote it is maid off. Enswer correctly to the point. Do not contridict your costimer. Do not taulk to loud— olways in a fine tune of voice.

Never knock your competitor regardless. Taulk only about your own product. Present yourself as such in this manner, then your prospactive costimer you will notice will become more and more interested in your product.

Never get exited when a costimer critises your merchandise. If he critises on certin things of your product dont get engry. The oposit. Act accordingly with a smile. Be convinsing and be humbil. Do not give a chance the costimer to get mad. Keep him smiling.

As you wolk in to your prospactive costimer you must look at him and size him up in the sper of the moment his nature. She or he rite there or then. When you say Good morning, and the costimer uproching you, that is the time to size up his or her nature. You must deside the type of charecter in your own miend. Whether he's uprobt or kind you have to deside in the moment of your How do you do. When oll of this is salved, and if you will fowlow up oll of this points, your helf of the battle is over. If you merchandise stands up to heff of your competitors your sale is maid.

Never go away engry, if you dont make for the first time a sale. Olways go away with a smile and dont get tierd and say The hell with him. Dont pass him up. Let the costimer get tierd as you coll on him or she again and again. As long as he or she are prospactive costimers coll on them as often as you can and befor long they will get so tierd that eventuly they will make a good costimer for you. In a long run you will be the winner. I am only giving you my own expirence as a Sailesmen. You will be sucsesful if you will make first a frend, then a costimer.

Remember one thing: frendship first, costimer second.

In a long run when you establisht oll the facts off my expirence, you will be the sucses. It wont hurt if you invite the costimer for lunch at times.

You olso must be dressd neet. Not sloppy. Clean shirt. Matching tie. Sout clean and prest. Oll of this things helps.

Whether conditions never stopt me to coll on a costimer. Raine, snow or shine never stopt me. Usully in the morning you will find oll the sailesmen congragate in the lobbie at the hotel shmousing, talking, telling storys, oll kind of nonsince. But I never pertisapait in this kind of conversation. You are waisting time. The morning is too valible to waist. If the whether is bad that is the time you will find your prospactive costimer in the office.

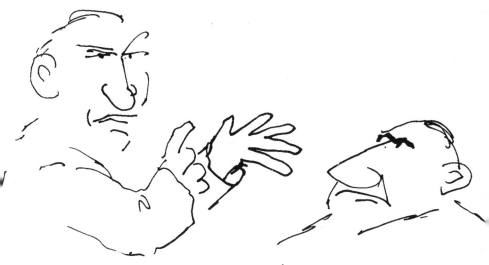

Do not tire out your costimer . . . .

137

Sure enoff, when I came in the costimer was very happy that in that misrable whether somebody had gutz enoff to com in. Must of the time my comming was very profitable. Well, this is to show you. Dont stay in the lobbie and tell storys. Go out regardless of work and whether. Your costimer will respect you more.

One more thing. I want to remine you not to discuse any politicks with your costimer. Safe your time. Your time is very costly. Come to the point whote you are efter. Taulk about your product. That will be your accomplishment.

Do not tire out your costimer with nonsens. By the time you will stard tulking about your product to *him* or *her* they will loose thair epitite. You are bound to loose a sale.

You olso must not forget that you as a sailesmen have very short working hours. You have only six working hours a day. A sailesmen cant stard working befor 9 A.M., up to 4 P.M. You cant coll on a costimer between 12 to 1:30 wich ectualie lives you 5½ to 6 hours a day. Becouse efter 4 or 4:30 P.M. you cant see nobody. By that time he or she is tierd. Murst of the time they wont look on anything.

By no mins do not get discorage if you dont make a sale. Carry on. Fight. If you loose one costimer in your territory ther are ten others to be pickt up. Ether way takit good nature.

One more thing. On the road stop in the best clean hotel. Eat the best food and enjoy life in your sper time. That will give you inspiration to carry on. On the road wile treveling no metter in whote dark alley you will be. Think. Dont be mislead. Think of your beautuful family you left at home. Your wife and your childrn . . .

I am giving you, Mr. Sailesmen, mine expirence in my long life that I went true. This lesson dont cost you anything. In fact if you will fowler this lesson you will gaine and that will help you in the older age as it helpt me. The world of your commodity will respect you and reconise you as a Pro. in your filld.

139

# ‹25›

## CHEPTER OF EXPIRENCE WITH A HAT COMPANY

At one time that I was a manufacture I was manufacturing milliner ornaments and I was catering to millinery manufactures. Thus days it was a big bussines. In Chicago alone there have been 125 manufactures of laidies hats. At that time I had my factory in the Millinery Bulding on Wecker Drive in Chicago. I was selling my ornaments oll over the Country. I didnt miss a one. Out side that I was manufacturing Costume Jewelry of hair ornaments such as Spanish combs and other accsessories oll of wich belong to laidies hair, I opend up a branch of making hat ornaments.

There was in Chicago at that time one millinery manufacture, the Ex Hat Company, a very large factory. I Sami could not sell them. No metter how hard I tried the enswer was No. They were very hi class people, very well off. But they were not perlite. In fact they were very cold to me. No Good Morning. Nothing. Just cold looks and no hello.

Well I gived up hopes and I stopped colling on this account. Efter oll I am human and rude people will hurt anyones fillings. They were so stiff.

Then one morning I came in to my office and oll of a sutten I got a telephone coll from the Ex Hat Company that I tried so hard to sell. They are comming over to see my line.

Very well. I was happy. They were frendly on the phone.

And they were frendly when they came. I was so surprised. They came over and they placed with me a very large order and they thankd me and they complimented me for the kind of such beautuful line I was manufacturing. In the millinery bussines the desighner is the boss on bying. No metter whotever I showd her, she boght. I was so happy that day, that day the Ex Hat Company finely placed with me such a beautuful order.

I worked with that company for about three months.

The first couple of months they paid me on time. On the

fourth month they went bankropt and they got me with $2,500.00.

That was a lot of money. Oll of a sutton they wouldnt taulk to me again. So then I knew that when they came to see me, they owed olredy a lot of money to thair other suppliers and they came to give me bussines when they were olredy in troble.

So they took me for a ride. Thus days that was a lot of money and they took me in a short time dooing bussines with that house. Ther was nothing I could do about it. It was for a wile a shock to me. I am a great optimist and I told myself it only hurts for a wile. I told myself Sami, never give up hopes. I told myself I would make up my losses som how, som times. No metter whote.

Finely, about four months efter the bankropty, I hear that Mr. Ex is back in bussines. He has opend a new factory. I figert out he must have new capital to stard again, but he was bank-ropt and he never paid his old creditors. Anaway he never paid me.

Right there I knew I will have a chence to make up my big loss if I will stard selling him again. I waited a week for him to coll me, but I didnt heard from him. Finely I went over to his place. He didnt coll me but I went.

They let me in his office and he was nise to me. Not so frendly as before, but not rude. I said to him

—Max, you know whote I came for.

He said

—Of course. Sami, I will introduce you to my desighner Hellen.

So he coled in the desighner Hellen and he was very grashous.

—Hellen, he said, This is Mr Silverman. He has very nise ornaments for hats. So whotever you can by from him, he will appreshiate it.

He was very grashous for somone who owed me $2500.00.

In the main time I turned to Hellen and I said, olso grashous

—Hellen, on this ocasion Id like to selebrate and take you to dinner tomorrow nite if it is O.K. with you.

So she said O.K. she would exsept my invitation. And Mr. Ex was smiling very heppy at both of us.

I came home and I said to my wife that I am taking out a young lady for dinner tomorrow nite and I explained her with whoem and wy. And whote my aim was. She understood.

—It is O.K. with me, my wife said to me.

The next nite I met Hellen and we went out to a nise restaurant. I olso gived her a nise present which she exsepted and everything went true beautuful. We became very good frends, and she as a desighner stardet to order goods from me olmost every other day.

In the main time I instructed in my factory that no one should deliver any merchandise to thair place. I will deliver by myself. I put a block of paper under the blotter on my desk and I marked the amount of money that I lost to the above consurn. The $2500.00.

144

Every time I delivered merchandise to that consurn I useto put extra $25 or $30 to my bill. In other worts, if Hellen ordered two gross I markd on the bill 2½ gross. She never checked the amount. She sighned the resipt and I wrote on my paper under the blotter the extra amount, that they paid me that much they owed me.

The only way I woold get my money.

I carried this on for about five months until I so that it richt the fool amount of the $2500. I was payed back and my loss was recoverd. I did not want any more money from that consurn. In fact I was a little beat engry with them for snubbing me oll that time and then comming to me when they noo they whore in finnancial troble. And then to act so grashous like nothing heppened. So I told them I would not ship them any more merchandise. Hellen came into the office and wanted to taulk to me. She esked me a lot of questions wy I woold not deliver any more merchandise to them.

I told her I got hurt with them ones and I was wery nervis about dooing much bussines with them again and that was final.

Mr Ex did not coll me at oll to find out whoet was the troble. Any way in the main time I got my money back and recovered my loss.

# ‹26›

## THE 50 HOUR EPESODE

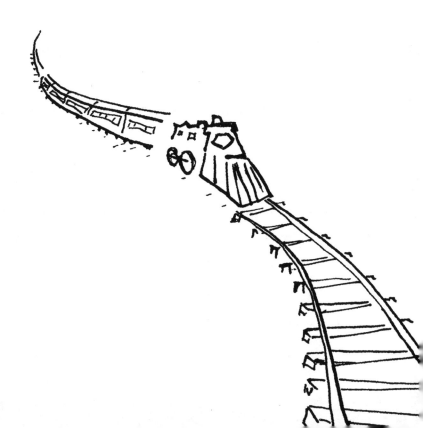

A sailesmen can have a lot of experences that are not so funny treveling oll over the Country. Off course you can have fun in your sper time. Som time. Not oll the time. Som time you can take out som young lady for dinner and spand an enjouyable evening not to get longsome, espacialy on a Saterday or Sonday. No one will blaime you for having a good time ones in a weil when the opertunity arises but in the maine time you should not forget the wife and childrn that you left behind you.

Ones I went on a very long trip to San Francisco. We stopped over in lots of places—St. Louis, Kansas City, Omaha, Denver. This one time I stopped off in Oakland, California to see costimers and then got back on the train to go to San Francisco. I so costimers dooing the day and treveled at nite on a couch—no slipers for me. My mottor was

—Never tiered. Slept oll nite on the train.

And olways redy to go to work in the morning. That was my pride and joy.

On this trip from Oakland to San Francisco the train stopped in the middle of the nite. Everybody was tier sleeping in the coach on a chair. Finely the conductor came in. Everbody was esking him

—Whote is the troble?

The conductor enswered.

—Ladies and gentlemen—we had a wash out.

In the morning about seven o'clock was daylite. And looking out the window the hole little town we were in was coverd from the river full of water. From the beginning people liked to make a joke of it, but it was really quite sereas. Lockyle the injuneer puled the train up on a hill to save the pessendgers from drowning. But the intire city was under water. Thair was hardly any food on the train.

—We really dont know how long we will stay heer, the conductor said. We will keep you oll informed. We might stay heer a couple of days. Dont be alarmed. We are quite safe here.

There was exsietment from the women and childrn.

—How about food? They asked the conductor.

—Well, we coled San Francisco and true halecopter they will drop in food to the train so dont worry. Thanks God we are safe.

Finely we got food. Oll kinds of sandwiches and coffee dropped in from the halocopters.

In the main time everybody was bored and tierd sitting and waiting until the train will stard moving again. Well, for Sami was a picknik. I tried to figur out how to keep the woomen in good humor.

I got ahold of a big card board and I maid a big sighn

HAIR DRESSER PARLORS.
MANICURE AND MASSURE.
PRISE FOR THE HOLE JOB ¢50.

Well, when oll the woomen saw that sighn dont ask the lefter and the kidding around whote was going on. They stayd in line to be next.

Naturly I was murst interested in certin costimers. First they had to be *zaftig* so I would not break their bones wile I do the massaging. Second they had to be fair good looking. Woomen

**149**

stardet comming in from the other couches to be massaged. In fact I had to give out numbers. It became a riet to get their turn next. The car where I had my Beauty Parlor was pact full of men and women.

One woomen wile I gave her a massage on her back she fell aslip. I thoght for a wile she fainted.

—Oh, she said, this is wanderful. I never had it so good.

Oll I can tell you my bussines was profitable. I dont need to tell you wich way? . . .

Well, as for my self I had a good time and oll of the people on the train said they will never forget this kind of enjoyment on the trip. And with that the conductor came in and told us the good news, that we are starding to move. As far as I am consurn I was wishing the train should have stayed for another 48 hours. Outside that I had a good time I olso had a good wacation.

We finely arrived in San Francisco and I Sami checkt into a hotel. I coled on my costimers with my 2 sample cases of costume jewelry. I got thrue in San Francisco, took the next train to Seattle, then Portland, Los Angeles, Minneapolis, Milwaukee and then home. I had with me some addresses the woomen gave me so they can in future rezoom the Good Time they had with Sami on the train.

150

# ‹27›

## CHEPTER OF OLL KINDS OF TROBLES DOOING THE WAR

Dooing the second World War the government confascated oll the metal in the Country. They needit the metal for amonition Manufactures in Providence stoped making metal ear rings. It became a shortedge of materials oll over the Country. The jobers of the Costume Jewlery would by olmost anathing to help their bussines.

One of the biggerst problems was getting stones. I mean Rhinestones. They were very important in Costume Jewelry. And dooing this war they were not avalible. In fact Svorovskie in ChecoSlovakie, the great Rhinestone manufacture and the suplier to oll the importers in the United States, could not deliver any Rheinstones to nobody. They only put everybody on a loutmen.

*ae oll worked together Taking out the stones*

I had a lot of troble desighning my hair ornaments without rhinestones. I stardet to advertise in oll papers for old dresses of any kind with trimmings of rhienstones. I askt anyone with

152

these dresses to bring them to my office of my factory and I would buy the dresses and take out the stones and use them for Costume Jewelry.

I got so many stones from so many places that I was able to supply other manufactures that were making Costume Jewelry. One morning wile I was in my office a young men came in. He said to me that he found our name in the phone book the ART COMB ENGRAVING CO., and that he has ten jackets fool with rhienstones wich it belongs to Sonia Hannie, the ice skater. He was her meneger.

So I boght oll ten jackets from him for $50. a jacket. There was sewed on this jackets a thousand gross of stones.

I took the jackets home and my hole family and oll the woomen from the naberhood set don with me and we oll worked together taking out the stones, from the little prongs. We had a little tweezer and some little knifes.

We took out oll the stones and cleand them and I took them to New York. I sold theses stones for $10.00 a gross to the manufactures there and they were very glad to pay that.

153

# >28<

## WOOLWORTHS

Another interesting insident heppend to me dooing the war with this stroggle to get rhinestones. Also the War #2.

Thus days, about 1942, we useto stop in New York at the Martinique Hotel, 32nd and Broadway. That was the center of the Costume Jewelry. Every jober, wholesaler and every Costume Jewlery sailesmen stoped at the Martinique Hotel. The meneger from the hotel maid everybody filling goot like home. His name was Mr Jhonson. Very kind and good nature. It was a regeler stock market. The jobers useto by and the sailesmen sold.

One day a frend of mine invited me to come to his home for dinner. He lived in New York. I excepted the inventation. That evening I got drest and took the subway to 96th St. As I got out from the subway I notised a Woolworths department store. In the window was displaid full with rhinstone pins. Prise ¢25.

I wolked into the store and I askt for the meneger.

—Yessir. Whote can I do for you?

—Yes, I repleid. I would like to by oll the pins you have on hand that you have in the window with the stones in them. How manny have you in stock and how much will you make it if I take the intire stock?

—No, he repleid. Woolworth dont make any spacial prise. And by the way whoet do you need this for?

I lit up my cigar.

—We are running a bazar at mine church, I said. I need this to give away for door prises.

—Can you use that manny pins?

—How manny have you in stock?

—About three thousand pins.

—I will take oll you have.

I knew very well it wont take me long to dispose of them. My costimers would be glad to get it. So Woolworths pact up the intire stock. I payed and I got a resept for same. I was

157

thanking in my hat that some other Woolworth stores must have the same pins with the rheinstones. So I askt the meneger to give me the names and addresses hoo has the same murchandise. By that time I forgot oll about my dinner date and I took the stock in a cab to my hotel.

The next day I did the same thing and I boght more pins from the other Woolworths. I filled up my intire room. My bed was so full with pins that I could hardly find room to sleep in my bed.

The fowloring morning I took som samples in my pocket and I said to my self Well, Sami get out and do som bussines.

I went don in the lobby for brackfest. The first costimer I uprocht was olso a little men with a big cigar. He is the kind of men that cant taulk with out swerring.

—You S.O.B., he said wen he so me, whote do you want? You must have something under your sleve.

—Yes. I have, I said.

In one way he was ruff. Yet on the other hand he was kind and olways had a smile on his face.

I showd him the pins.

—You S.O.B. (again) Sami, haumuch do you want for the pins?

—Six dollars a dozen, I said.

—Haumanny have you got?

—I have about 50 gross.

—You have! he said. I shell take 25 gross. Ship them to me at ones.

I told him I will.

The rest of the pins I sold to a jober in Chicago. That was a very profitable week for Sami.

# ⇁29⇁

## ANOTHER INCEDENT

I remember another World War #2 incident that heppend that is unforgetable. Again I was in New York. I was wolking on 37th St. I had a frend who had a store there. He was in the button bussines, an importer. Casualy I was standing in front of his store tulking to him. And wile we were tulking he said to me

—Sami, do you know anybody can use some small fire polish stones oll colors?

—Let me see whote you have, I said.

We went into his store on the ground floor of a big building. He opend a cabinet and ther I saw about 25 thousand gross fire polish stones in the original packages wich it goes 10 gross in a package. Fire polish stones are the cheapest grade of stones. But you couldnt get first quality stones or any grade dooing the war.

—Haumuch do you want for it? I said to him.

—I will take whote I paid for it. I paid ¢3 a gross.

—Very well. Give me right now a couple of packages.

I took this samples and I said to him that I will let him know.

In this same building I knew of one manufacture that was making Costume Jewelry. He was on the twelfth floor. I went up in the elevator to this manufacture and I showed him the stones.

—Haumanny have you? He esked me.

I said about twenty-five thousand gross.

—Haumuch?

—If you can use the intire lot I will sell it for ¢15 a gross, I said.

He didnt bet an iie.

—Can you make it a little cheaper? he said.

—No, I said. Thats it.

He boght the intire lot. Late in the efternoon I came back to my frend donstairs and I boght the lot for ¢3 a gross and I delivered in the same bulding on the twelfth floor oll the stones for ¢15 a gross.

¢ a gross, I said.

He didnt bet an iie

are included with each Set

① For full permanent: Part hair in center. For each curl take strand of hair about 1 in. wide, 2 in. deep from hairline, draw through felt protector and side opening of metal protector.

② Moisten strand of hair with wave solution. Place between 2 pieces of cloth on curler, roll hair smoothly up to metal protector. Bend wire ends of curler to hold curl in place.

③ After winding 8 curls, moisten flannel attached to cellophane, bend cellophane over curl. Shape carefully to fit curl tightly. Place spring pinch clips over first four curls.

④ Insert Infra-Red heating tubes in first 2 special hollow clips, leave for 6 min., pull tubes out and place in next 2 curls. After 8 curls are finished continue until all are made.

## New **INFRA-RED** Ray Home Perm

### Smart Kurl brings you New Way to make softer, quic in just 6 minutes...preserves natural luster, vitality of

Now Smart Kurl brings you an entirely *new* method of giving you beautiful, long-lasting permanent wave *at home*. By means of a special Red Ray electric heat unit, curls full head of hair in less than 2 hrs. harm natural, lustrous beauty of hair. Heat from Infra-Red tubes right to make soft, natural looking curls; last until hair grows out. for adding a few curls quickly. Makes 2 curls in just 6 minutes! Set gi permanent. Includes: plastic handle with cord, 2 Infra-Red Ray spring clips, 8 curlers, 8 felts, 8 metal protectors, 2-ounce wave solu pads, instruction folder. Equipment lasts years; just buy refill unit volt, AC or DC current. 35 watt. Satisfaction guaranteed or money

**25 K 9511E—Smart Kurl Infra-Red Wave Set.** Shpg. wt. 2 lbs. 6 oz. (5c Fe
**25 K 9512E—Refill Set.** 2 ounce permanent wave solution, 24 cellopha Shipping weight 1 pound. (5c Federal Tax included)................
**25 K 9513—Replacement Tubes.** Heat more than 300 hours. Use with Smart-Kurl Wave Set, 25K9511E. Shipping weight 2 ounces.........

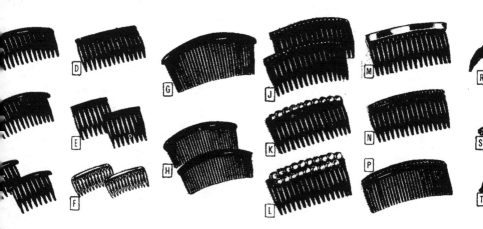

## S .. to add a glamorous touch to your hair style ... fashion right, smart

rip Tooth Combs. Hold hair securely, com-
nooth plastic. *Colors* shell, amber, gray.
—4¾x1½-inch Back Comb. Lies close *Please state color.* Shpg. wt. 1 oz. Each **9c**
—4x1½-inch Side Comb. Keeps hair *Please state color.* Shpg. wt. 1 oz. Each **9c**
—2½x1½-inch Tuck Combs. Handy size air-dos. *State color.* Shpg. wt. 1 oz. Pr. **9c**

"Grip-Tuth" Hair-tainer. Thinner, lighter. le in hair. Slip in place easily, stay in. tic. *Colors* shell, amber, crystal.
—1⅝x1⅝-inch Hair-tainers. Favorite for weeps. *State color.* Shpg. wt. 1 oz. Ea. **23c**
—1½x1⅝-inch Hair-tainers. Handy ctive. *State color.* Shpg. wt. 1 oz. Pr. **23c**

"Midget" Combs. 1x1⅞-inch. For short children's fine hair. Shpg. wt. 1 oz. tate shell, amber, gray.......... Pair **9c**

"Kant-Slip" Straight Tooth Combs. Handy aids for well groomed hair. Made of smooth molded plastic.
**G** 25K9406—4¾-inch Back Comb. *State color* shell, (brown), amber, or gray. Shpg. wt. 1 oz. Ea. **9c**
**H** 25K9407—3⅛-inch Side Comb. *State color* shell, (brown), or amber. Shipping weight 1 oz. Pr. **9c**

Ornamental Combs. Add a finishing touch to your glamorous up-sweep. Extra charm for your long bob. Lovely. fashionable accent for day or evening wear.
**J** Nailhead Beauty. Row nailheads on Grip Tooth 3½-in. plastic comb. *State* gold, silver color nail-heads. Shpg. wt. 2 oz.
25K9600E—Shell color comb............. Pair **54c**
Lustrous Lovely. What could be more feminine to tuck into your curls than this dainty comb richly studded with glowing imitation pearls! Set on shell color plas-tic Grip Tooth Comb. Stays in place. 3½ in. wide. Made with 1 or 2 rows pearls.
**K** 25 K 9601E—With one row Imitation Pearls. Shpg. wt. 2 oz....................Each **58c**
**L** 25K9602E—With two rows Imitation Pearls. Shpg. wt. 2 oz....................Each **98c**

**M** Classically Smart. Gold or silver shell color plastic Grip Tooth 25 K 9603E—3½ inches wide. *Pleas* Shipping weight 2 ounces........
**N** Dazzling Splendor. Sparkling ro rhinestones deep-set on Grip 25 K 9604E—3½ inches wide. Shell Shipping weight 2 ounces........
**P** Matchless Magic. 26 brilliant stones deep-set on straight too 25 K 9605E—4 inches wide. Shipping weight 2 ounces........
**R** Graceful and Glamorous. Love straight tooth plastic comb d quality rhinestones. Shpg. wt. 2 o 25K9606E-3½ in. wide. Shell color c
**S** Glistening Curl Catcher. 11 rhin narrow top shell barrette with 25K9607E—2½ in. long. Plastic. Shp
**T** Star-Bright Barrette. Beveled at 32 first quality deep-set rhineste 25 K 9608E—2 in. long. Shpg. wt.

# ‹30›

## NEVER BRAKE A PROMISED

There is olways a time olmost ones in five years that in the Costume Jewelry one idum gets hot and you cant hardly deliver to your costimers the amount they need. No metter how much goods you have on hand it is not enoff.

This heppend efter the war with luside beads, 20 mm. 60 inch ropes. This idum was so hot that three good jobers could have used my intire output. I had a surce of getting this idum and making a risonable profit off same. At that time I pickt out the 12 best jobers to give them the ropes, and they paid cash on delivery. Berns and Friedman was one of my dear costimers.

I knew Hi Friedman when he was working for Morris Mann and Riley. He was a sailesmen for them, and wile he was on the road he met up with another sailesmen by the name Bill Burns. Bill Burns was a flower sailesmen and he and Hi Friedman desidet to go into the flower bussines together. They were together about a couple of years, but maid no progress.

In the maintime I Sami wolked into Hy's place because I knew him from Morris Mann and Riley.

—Hi Hy. How are you dooing?

—Not so hot. It looks like we will give this up.

Just at that time Costume Jewelry was starding to go very well. I said to him

—Why dont you stard in the Costume Jewelry? And I will help you.

—You will?

I had at that time olredy my own factory.

—Yessir. I shell do oll I can.

And I did. I maid up spacial goods for him. I useto by off plastic buttons and paist in plastic ear wires—thus days ther wore no metal ear wires, because the government stoped oll the brass and metal to manufacture for Costume Jewlery. That was dooing the war #2 again. So they maid plastic. Every morning I useto deliver to his place ear rings loose, on no cards. I useto throw in a box 5 gross and bring the ear rings to his place. And he paid ¢4 a dz. He was very happy with me. His bussines stardet to progress and I maid a good profit.

Dooing the war there was shortedge of oll kinds of goods, but for Hy I did the best I could. There was no shortedge for Burns and Friedman if I could help it.

There was a shortedge in pearl necklaces. I hepend to find in a Baisment about 50 gross of pearls. But they whore discolored and dirty, olmost black.

Imidiately I went to Hi.

—Hy, can you use this?

—I sure can.

He boght the entire lot.

One time I went to Leominster. I boght fifty barrels of wooden beads and I strung long ropes out of wooden beads spacial for Burns Friedman.

So you can see of oll my costimers Burns Friedman came first. Hy was a dear frend of mine. So when ther was this big run on luside beads in ropes and they were so hard to get I promised to deliver him 1000 dz weekly and so I did. A promis is a promise. I Sami never broke my promise.

At that time my son Lloyd was working for me just efter he came out of the army. I had to go to New York and I coled my son Lloyd over to me. I said to him

—Lloyd, weil I am away you take over to Burns & Friedman this 2000 dz of ropes or whotever we have on hand when the shipment will arrive.

—O.K. Daddy, I will, Lloyd says to me.

And I left for New York. Lloyd was very agresive and he wanted to show me that he can get much more money than the prise I was getting from Burns & Friedman, or any of the jobbers. He was sure that I would be very happy about that.

So he takes a sample of the ropes and he goes over to Marshell Field and Co. and he asks to see the byer from the jewelry dept. This is strictly retail of course.

She wolks up to him.

—Young men, you want to see me?

—Yes mem, I do.

And he takes out the rope of luside beads from his pocket.

—Can you use this?

Her ies popt out wen she so the rope.

—Wher did you get this?

—This is my Daddys. He has plenty of stock on hand.

—How manny can you deliver?

—Well, we have at present about 2000 dz.

—How much?

—That will cost you $14.50 a dz.

One thing he new quite well, that Burns & Friedman paid his father much less. In fact we sold to them that idum at that time for $9.00 a dz. So he Lloyd my son was trying to make more money.

In the main time the byer said to him

—Just a minut. Stay right here. I shell come rite back.

She went over to consolt with the merchandise men to get

166

the approval to by the 2000 dz. It didnt take five minutes. She came back.

—Sonny, how quick can you deliver?

—Tomorrow morning I will deliver the entire stock at $14.50 a dz.

—O.K. Heer is an order for the goods.

The next day he took a little hand truck with another helper and wealed in that little hand truck direct to Marshal Field in the jewelry dept. The byer olmost fainted to see oll of the 2000 dz delivered as promised right on the floor.

—O.K., young men, she said. Try to get us another shipment next week.

Lloyd was very happy about this sale. Asspacialy that he got five dollars and fifty cents more on the dozen than his daddy got.

At the end of the week I came home from New York. Lloyd greated me with a big smile.

—Well, sonny, the shipment came in on time?

—Yessir.

—Did you delivert the ropes to Berns and Friedman?

He looks at me still with a smile.

—No ser, I did not.

—Whoet heppend?

—I sold the 2000 dz to Marshall Field and we got $14.50 a dz instead of $9.00 a dz.

For a minut I had to sidaren, not knowing whote hit me.

Efter I was sitting for a couple of minuts, I said to my super sailesmen son

—You broked my promised. I am not interested in haumuch money extra I was making. Again—

—You broked my Promise. I maid a warble Promise to my best costimer and long time costimer and frend that I will deliver this goods to him. Not to Marshall Filld.

Finely I have the strangth to stend up. I said

—Sonny. Ones you make a promis in your future life keep the promis. Never never do it again. A contract you can ter up. But a Promis you cant brake it. Again a promis is not a pees of paper. Your mout maid a promised. Let it be a lesson to you for your future life. Som day you will grow up a young bussinesmen and you will understand better.

With that I closed my conversation with my son and the next morning I went back to New York to make an arengement to fulfill my Promise for the intire order to Berns & Friedman.

This ends my story. Not to brake a Promise.

# THE STYLE OF HAIR ORNAMENTS WENT OUT OF STYLE
## 1950

**Side Combs**
Good-looking, polished celluloid. Smooth finished teeth hold firmly. Length, 4¼ in. Colors: Shell or Amber. State color. Shipping weight, 2 ounces.
**25 D 9060**
Per Pair......**21c**

**Rhinestone Set**
1 Back Comb, 4½ in. 2 Side combs, 4 in. Brown Shell or Amber celluloid. State color. Shpg. wt., 2 oz.
**25 D 9029**
Set of three.....**41c**
**25 D 9028**—Set of 3 (as above) without stones..........**25c**

**Back Combs**
Sparkling white stones, set in polished celluloid. Brown shell color. Length, 4¼ in.
Shipping weight, 2 ounces.
**25 D 9023**
Each..........**23c**
**25 D 9024**
Plain (no stones)..**15c**

**Brown Combs**
Smoothly polished celluloid. Shell color. Handsome and useful. Back comb, 4½ in. Side combs, 4 in. Shipping weight, 2 oz.
**25 D 9015**
Back Comb. Each.**9c**
**25 D 9014**
Side Combs. Pair.  **9c**

**4-in. Gray Back Comb**
**25 D 9054**  **29c**
Stone Set. Each.
**25 D 9053**
No Stones. Each.**23c**

**3½-in. Side Combs**
**25 D 9055**  **39c**
Stone Set. Pair.
**25 D 9056**
No Stones.  Pr...**27c**
Shpg. wt., each, 2 oz.

After aperating my bussines on Milwaukee Ave. I found that the place became too small. Then I moved don ton on Monroe between Franklin and Market Street. The address there was 317 W. Monro on the 5th floor. I had the intire floor, 1000 squer feet. I had 50 people working for me. The name of the ART COMB ENGRAVING CO. was knowing from cost to cost. I traveled oll over the Country to sell to the wholesalers of the Costume Jewelry my own merchandise.

I had with Sears and Roebuck two pages of combs and barrets in their catalogue. I gained confidence and trust amongst my costimers. I was humbold and kind to the smaller costimer as well as to the larger accounts. And finely efter working sucsesfully for manny years—working very hard—my sucses of my bussines came to an end. It came to me as a surprise. The style of woomens hair ended. They stardet cutting their hair short. Long hair no more. Ther was no room to hold the ornaments on to the hair.

One morning I came in to my factory esusual. My hobby was when ever I came in to the factory I olways went in first in the shop and went to every table . . . Good morning to everyone. Then I went in to the office, oppening up my mail. I wasnt looking for orders. It was a queshion hoo to send first the merchandise.

As I was sitting in my office the first telegram came from Sears Roebuck . . .

CANSEL ALL ORDERS ON HAND. HOLD FOR FURTHER NOTISE.

I had two color pages with Sears. For a moment I was thanking Thanks God, that will give me a chence to catch up with the rest of my costimers.

But befor long when it came up to more time manny manny more telegrams came in. KINDLY CANSEL ALL ORDERS ON HAND UNTIL FURTHER NOTISE.

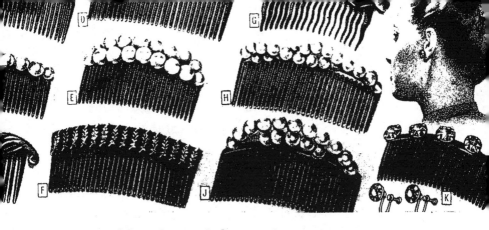

# ook young and lovely with bewitching Hair Ornaments

ornamental comb into your hair to put a finishing touch to your glamorous up-sweep or add charm to your long bob. There's a very occasion and outfit . . . for daytime or evening wear. You'll look ever so stylish and lovely with a decorative comb in your hair.

w of tiny metal
nell-color plas-
gold-color or
2 oz.
ncl.) Pr. 54¢

lustrous white
in. shell-color
, 2 oz.
incl.) Ea.28¢

ll (mottled lt.
n. comb.
z.:..Ea. 28¢

**D Unusually Pretty.** Charmingly different . . . 1 row of shiny gold-color metallized beads on shell-color plastic comb. Lovely when worn with the very popular new gold costume jewelry. 3½-inch comb. Shpg. wt. 2 oz.
25E9682E—(20% Fed. Tax incl.) Ea.58¢

**E Fashion Perfect.** Exquisite for gala occasions . . . daytime or evening. 2 rows of gleaming white imitation pearls on shell-color plastic comb. 3 inches wide. Shpg. wt., 2 oz.
25E9683E—(20% Fed.Tax incl.) Ea.58¢

**F Attractive and Different.** 15 fine gold-color metal leaves on black band . . . mounted on 3½-inch shell-color plastic comb. Shipping wt., 2 oz.
25E9684E—(20% Fed. Tax incl.) Ea.58¢

**G Lovely Bow Knot.** Decoration and comb made of demi-shell (mottled lt. brown) plastic. 3 in. wide.
25 E 9456—Shpg. wt., 2 oz. Ea. 79¢

**H Flattering Twist.** 2 rows of white imitation pearls on 3¾-inch shell-color plastic comb. Shpg. wt., 4 oz.
25E9692E—(20% Fed. Tax incl.) Ea.96¢

**J Glamorous Effect.** 2 rows of white imitation pearls are across the back of 3½-inch s plastic comb. Shpg. wt., 4 oz.
25E9685E—(20% Fed.Tax incl.)

**K Comb and Earring Set.** La lated jewels on 3 in. plast Matching jewels on gold-colo screw-type earrings. State color aqua green, emerald green, blue, rose. (20% Fed. Tax incl.)
25E9613E—Shpg. wt., 4 oz. Se
25E9614E—Shpg. wt., 2 oz.

### Narrow-Top Twin Barrettes

**L** An ideal barrette for children's hair because it's so narrow and dainty looking. Also used by many grownups. Stay-tight metal clasp holds hair securely so barrette cannot slip. Made of shell-color (brown) plastic. 2 inches long. Shipping weight, 1 oz.
25 E 9410 . . . . . . . . . . . . . . . Pair 9¢

### Graceful Twin Bow Barrettes

**M** Wear them in colors to match or harmonize with your dresses. Made of lightweight plastic with stay-tight metal clasp which holds hair securely. Solid bow, 2¼ inches long. *Colors:* amber, shell (brown), red, white or blue. *State color.* Shpg. wt., 1 oz.
25 E 9412 . . . . . . . . . . Pair 9¢

### Oval Shaped Barrette

**N** Attractive and different . . . a charming ornament for your or your child's hair. Made of lovely demi-shell (mottled light brown) color plastic. Oval shape with open center . . . very effective when worn in pairs. 2½ inches long. Shipping wt., 1 oz.
25 E 9416 . . . . . . . . . . . . . . . Each 23¢

### Curl Catcher Barrette

**P** Exquisite and feminine for gala or everyday occasions. 5 gleaming imitation white pearls on a 2-inch plastic barrette. Shpg. wt., 3 oz.
25E9689E—(20% Fed.Tax incl.) Ea.28¢

### Bow-knot Back Barrette

**R** Graceful cutout bow-knot made of fine molded plastic. Holds hair firmly . . . wear it as a back barrette on long bobs. Size: 5¼ inches long. *Colors:* amber, shell (brown), red, white, or blue. *Please state color wanted.* Shipping wt., 1 oz.
25 E 9413 . . . . . . . . . . . . . . . Each 9¢

### Back Barrette

**S** Holds your hair securely and neatly in place. Made of molded plastic . . . demi-shell (mottled lt. brown) color. Long buckle shape with pointed ends.

### Ornamental Barrette

**T** Glamour galore when you wear this stunning barrette. 11 lustrous imitation white pearls on lovely, daisy design plastic barrette . . . it will add a stylish and lovely touch to your long bob. Tiny teeth hold hair securely. It's handy, quick and convenient to wear barrettes instead of hairpins. About 6 inches long. Shipping weight, 4 ounces.
25 E 9690E—(20% Federal Tax included) . . . . . . . . . . . . . . Each 83¢

### "Kant-Slip" Combs

It will be easy to keep hair in sleek hair-dos all day long with matching Kant-Slip combs. Use large comb for center back in an upsweep . . . side combs will keep short ends in place. Smooth plastic. *Colors:* gray, shell (brown), amber (reddish yellow). *Please state color wanted.* Shipping weight, each, 1 ounce.
**U** 25 E 9406—Back Comb. 4¾-inch width . . . . . . . . Each 14¢
**V** 25 E 9407—Side Comb. 3¼-inch width . . . . . . . . Pair 10¢

### "Grip-Tuth" Combs

First aid for straggly ends . . . keeps them in place and helps make your upsweep look neater. Large back comb or tuck combs; made of molded plastic. Grip-Tuth combs hold securely. *Color:* shell (brown), amber, crystal. *Please state color wanted.*
**W** 25 E 9400—Back Comb. 2¾-in. width. Shpg. wt., 1 oz. Ea. 23¢
**X** 25 E 9403—Tuck Combs. 1⅝-in. width. Shpg. wt., 1 oz. Pr. 23¢

### "Grip-Tuth" Shortee Combs

**Y** Just the thing for those very short ends. Keeps them in place . . . holds hair securely. Ideal for children's fine hair. *Colors:* shell (brown), amber, crystal. *Please state color.*
25 E 9404—1¾ inches wide.
Shipping wt., 1 oz. . . . . . . Pair 23¢

Buy on Sears Easy Payment Plan. It's

By that time I began to understand my truble. I relised the style of combs is out and my $5000.00 stock is worthlest.

Long distens telephone coles came in from Leominster, Mass. from my creditors. They olso new of the truble and they tryed to comfort me. In fact the intire Leominster became on a stand still.

I imediatly laid off all my help from my shop and I tried to salvidge my stock so I can pay off my creditors. Butt no mether whote I tried . . . No Go. The style is out, and that was the finish of my sucses. I sure found myself in distress and uncomfortable knowing that yesterday I was a rich men and today I am a poor men.

A couple weeks later wile I was still trying to sell out, a men coled me on the phone.

—Mr Silverman, I am comming in to see you. Will you be in your office?

—Whote is it about?

—Never mind, the men said to me on the other side of the phone. When I come I will explaine to your adventage.

—O.K. I said. Come over.

Finely ther comes in a big men. I knew then ther must be someting phonny. To me he lookd like a Hoodlom.

—O.K. Mister, I said. Whoets on your mine?

—Mr Silverman, we know that you bussines is out. Your style of merchandise is out. You cant get nothing for it. We know that you are carrying a large Insurance policy. If you

172

livit to us, we will deliver full amount of the Insurance. We have the protection for you in every way. Al you have to do is to give us a key to your place and wolk away. We will take care of the rest.

—But tell me, whote are you going to do?

—We will put *Pine apple. Bam.*

—And haumuch do you want for this job?

—$5,000.00.

—O.K. Mister, I said. Let me do some thanking and to deside. I will let you know.

That day and that nite I was wauking back and fort. *Whoet to do.* Finely I came to my desision not to exsept that proposition. Supose I am cought and go to jail? I wont be able to suport my wife and childrn. But if I Sami am a free man I olways will be able to take care of my family somhow. Besides that I dont want the conshes on my had. I want to be a free man, and to do the right thing. Yes. This is my desision.

NO.

In my mine I know that I will olways make a leaving for my wife and childrn.

The next day the hoodlom coled me regarding my desision.

—Gentlemen, the enswer is NO.

And with that I stardet to salvegh my inventory and the meashinery I sold for whote I could get wich was olmost nothing. I sold myself the intire stock in Mexico. Off corse I realised very little for my stock. In fact I got for the intire factory 25% off the dollar. But I was able to slip well at nite and to think how to take care of my family. And with this money I settled with the creditors.

As for my self I was olmost broke. At the time that I went into the bussines of manufacturing Hair Ornaments I was too young to understand that som time the product will be out of style. I was at that time in the age of 30. However by Sami never a doll moment and I begin thanking whote to do. How to make a livelihood for my dear family.

# ›32›

## CHEPTER OF MAKING DESSISIONS

I finely desidet to stard in Costume Jewelry as a holesaler, jobbing Costume Jewelry. Since I had stardet from my young days in that bussines, I felt that I'll be able to do it. Providence, R.I. was the prinsipil city to make castings with rhienstones and to make oll kind of Costume Jewelry. My name was still knowing in that field so I went to Providence and New York and stardet in Costume Jewelry as a jober under the name Lloyds Costume Jewelry. The reason for me picking that name is that Lloyd is my oldest son.

At that time Lloyd went to the wore and I felt when Lloyd will return from the wore he will have a redy going bussines and wouldnt need to look for a job. In the main time I olso took in my Son in low Martin who was maried to Bernice. I figered out by having two young men in the bussines I couldnt help to make a sucses by me having the know how whote to buy and styling and also with my good name among the creditors. I couldnt mis. You know whote? I did mis.

As much as I new about bying and to promote bussines on the out side I did not had the power to menege my own childrn in the bussines. I could buy the finest merchandise and styles and make up the sample lines and prising. I could make everything redy for the boyes to go out to see som costimers. At first they went out and sold and broght in som nise orders. I was very heppy. For a wile.

The fowloring week I notised the boys are staying in. They stayd in the office. They are drinking cocktails and taulking on the phone. By that time Howard and Lloyd were both back from the wore and oll three of them were in the office. They went out one day, two days, and stayd in the rest of the week. I said to them

—Boyes, whotes wrong? Why are you not going out to sell?

—Well, Daddy, we cant show the same costimer the same goods.

That was their enswer.

I said

—Boyes, there are thousands of costimers.

They said

—We need new desighns.

So I maid new desighns, new styles. They went out of town a little bit and then back to the office and the same thing. On Friday nite they took their checks, they drank cocktails. Our factory was on 325 So. Franklin St. We had a few employees.

By that time I notised that there will be another failure in my ingenuiti. I knew then that as a holesaler I will not be able to carry on and make a livlihood for my children and my self and family.

I finely maid my desision. I coled in the boys.

—Boys, I said, you are very young and you can make a livlihood for you self. I got to make a livelihood for my family.

And I did. I closed the bussines. Martin went back to the law, wich he should never have left it, and Lloyd went to work for somebody else in jewelry and finely moved to Los Angeles. Howard stayd with me. In fact he was my shadow.

The next day I went over to see my good frend Hi Friedman.

He was by that time a very sucsesful wholesaler. Hi Friedman and Jane Waters, his buyer, said to me

—Sami, come in with us in our place. You will make som merchandise for us.

So I did.

# ›33‹

## BERNS AND FRIEDMAN

I stayd with Berns and Friedman for about a year. They whore very nise people and very nise to me. At that time their company was at 210 W. Adams St. Kenneth Wolf was a sailesmen for them, a very bright men and is now helping to run the intire company. Anyway efter a wile I could see that working for Berns and Friedman is not going to work out for me. I was a desighner and I did styling but I new I didnt produce right for them.

I wanted to be the one who said I am going. I didnt want Hy and Jane Waters to feel they had to tell me. So I told them.

One night I stayd a little bit longer befor closing up. I came in to Hy Friedmans office and I said

—Hy, I am sorry to tell you, becaus I know oll the good things you have don for me. But I liked to quit this. I cant see any progress here for my future, I liked to do something that will make my life better for my livlihood.

Then Jane and Hy said to me

—Sami, whote would you liked to do?

Then I said to Jane, I coled her Jannie, she heppend to be a pretty smart girl

—I will tell you. I would liked to get som lines from factorys out of Providence to represent them.

—Thats a good idia, Jannie said.

Befor long she maid a few telephone coles in Providence from the factorys she was bying from and with that I stardet as a representative selling to the wholesale traid. It was no novelty for me selling. As long as I had my healt and my trade mark my cigar I olways could be a good sailesmen by being humbold and kind. I olways had a kind wort to anabody. Olways with a smile. I never carryed a gruge on annebody. My greeting to people was olways alike.

Anaway Berns and Friedman was a great help to me. Hy Friedman never forgot oll the things I did for him when he needed me. They helpt me become a representative for vereas lines wich was ideal for me. And I thoght since Howard my son is with me like a shadow anyway I will take him along when I am a representative and train him.

# >34<

## CHEPTER OF MY SON HOWARD

When I stardet to be a representative my son Howard was growing up to be a youngmen. Very quiat. Little bid on the shai side but very polite, gentile, and I thoght of him how he shuld become a men of the world. I desidet to take him with me in to the bussines so he shuld fowlor my experence and shuld lurn to become a good sailesmen. Olredy I gave up the Lloyds Costume Jewlery because it was not working out with Lloyd and Martin. But Howard I desidet to take as a partner in the selling organasation because he was so quiat and shai.

Dooing the few years that Howard was with me he desidet to get meried. He fond a charming younglady and befor long they got meried. Her name was Judy Rose. In fact I was very heppy about the meridge as I felt that will make him to try and work harder for his family.

184

Howard is today knowing from cost to cost

Befor long I notised that Howard did not have his own inishitive. I felt it is no good. He has got to stand on his own two fit. It botherd me so much. Not for me. I wanted him to be a sucses on his own. The quality was there. But so long as he was with me Howard moved behind me. It didnt work.

Lloyd was still in the jewelry line in California. I gave him money, a car, he should build his own life out there. But Howard was still with me, in my shadow.

Finely one morning I came to the office and I said to Howard.

—Howard, I am leaving you. Whotever lines we have in this office belongs to you. You be on your own and I will be for my self.

He was very startle.

—But Daddy, he said, whote will you do?

—I am more interested in you, Sonny. Dont worry for me. You are a youngmen. Make a start for youself.

That morning I wolked out. I left my son Howard alone.

People out on the out side thoght I was a min father to do a thing like that. I know they thoght so. I got word from that. But I wasnt min. I new the quality was there and the nowledge was there. I new that Howard and his family would suffer for a wile. And they did. They had a hardship for a few years. He was a little beat upset wen I left him. He had two smoll childrn. But he had to stand on his own two fit. There was nothing to taulk about it.

And you know whoet? I was rite.

I new dip in my hart with the nowledge and experence he has he will become befor long one of the great sailesmen of the country. He did. I new that in the time to come and with his behavyer and kindnes and gentile to the costimers he will be autstanding in his fild. And you know whote?

HE IS TODAY.

My son Howard is today knowing from cost to cost and loved by every jober in the country. He is loved by everyone he meets. I have today *nachas* that my son Howard is a master in the Costume Jewlelry trade. I am the proud father. His company is the Contemporary Import Co. He is olso a partner in Smart Creations, an importer in Chicago and Fashion Jewelry in Providence and he represents many many more.

My son Lloyd is working with my son Howard. Lloyd is covering the west coast for Howard. I am proud of both of them. Lloyd meried a wanderful girl Gloria who was a spich terepist. And they have two childrn Ellen and Lerry.

Howards wife Judy rased three beautuful daughters. And an interesting thing, Howards daghter Randie is lerning the Trade from Jane Waters at Berns & Friedman. She took up merchandising in colledge and she is lerning the Costume Jewelry. Her father doesnt need her, but Kenneth Wolf, who is very active at Berns & Friedman, does need her. So I am a proud father and a proud grandfather too. And the family is going on with the Costume Jewelry.

# >35<

## CHEPTER OF MY OWN LINES

Efter I wolked out from my son Howard I had to find my self new lines because as I said olredy I left everything we had with him. My ambition is to get lines from other manufactures in the fild of Costume Jewelry and to sell for them on a comition bases to the wholesalers, jobers of Costume Jewlry. I olways want to deal with wholesalers. Never ritailers. You cant play on both ends the fiddle. It is more profitable, you get bigger orders and there is less aggravation to deal with jobers. The byer at Marshall Filds is a personal frend of mine. He knows that I will never sell to them ritail. They pay more money, but you dont get the volume. I sold to Marshall Fillds wholesale, when they had a wholesale division near Carson Pirie Scott. They were olways very refined. They dint by as much as Carsons. But they were very perlite.

Off course when I left Howard my name was knowing oll over. The problem was to find lines that were not competitive becouse I could not sell lines that compete with one and other.

Finely I found four lines that I could represent with no trouble.

## PERFECT PEARL

The owner of that company, Perfect Pearl of Chicago coled me one morning that he would liked to see me. His name was Lio Gluck.

I came over to see him. He greeted me with a warem welcome.

—Whoet is on your miend? I esked.

—Sami, I would like that you should represent me for the Midwest.

—Mr Gluck, I said. You have a sailesmen for the Teritory.

—Yes, I know I have, Mr Gluck replied. But he dont want to trevel to cover that Teritory and I have desidet to let him go.

I would never take a line from a sailesman away. But Mr Gluck said to me

—Sam, I would let him go anaway.

Finely, going over, back and fort, I escepted. I closed a deal with Lio Gluck. Perfect Pearl imports necklaces, ear rings, pearls, mother of pearl pins, chain goods and gold and silver metal.

When I took over the line to work with my costimers many wholesalers in the Costume Jewelry hardly new of Perfect Pearl in Chicago as an importer. I Sami with hard work did not took very long to introduse this line oll over the Mid West. I took care of that line as if it would be my own bussiness.

In the later years Robert Gluck, Lio Gluck's son, stept into the bussines. In fact he took over the hole operation of the Perfect Pearl oll over the country. Robert I find intelegent and progressive. His father was a fine men bussines wise.

## FAIRDEAL MANUFACTURING CO.

Fairdeal Manifacturing Co. is in Providence, R.I. They fond out about me, that I am availible for the Mid West. They wrought me a letter if I would be interested to represent them for the Mid West. The letter was sighned by Morton Katz.

I coled Mr Katz by phone.

—Yes, he said, we are interested for you to represent us for your Teritory. You come to Providence and we will taulk things over. We will reimburst you your expence.

So I went to Providence and the same day we closed my relaitionship with Fairdeal to represent them for the Mid West. They make pins, chains and ear rings. They have nothing to do with imports. Everything they have is manufactured in Providence. So they do not compete with Perfect Pearl.

Mr Morton Katz, the general meneger of Fairdeal and Dick Serdjemian, the owner of that company, was pleast with me as one of them.

Beside of selling I was olso good of checking credit. To be a sailesmen not only selling merchandise but you are to know olso credit wise. In fact in my 70 years of experence my factory never lost any money from my accounts.

Of course there was no problem for me to sell thus manufactures products since I was selling the same costimers befor and I was knowing amoungst the trade as Sami Silverman. It wasnt to hard to do. Until to day I am still selling. But I am not treveling any more but attend four shows. Two shows in Providence and two shows in New York for the year.

My costimers give me the respect of my age. And as a Humble Sailesmen.

Fairdeal in Providence I had to resighn it as I could not do justis as I have given up treveling in the Mid West. And this is the respond in the Jewelry Magazine from this factory

**FASHION ACCESSORIES**  July, 1977

Let it be known
throughout the land

FAIRDEAL
MANUFACTURING CO.

unashamedly avows
their love for

SAM SILVERMAN

who has served
us nobly for
these many years —
and has with
great honor
thrown in the towel.

## ORIGINAL NOVELTY OF CHICAGO

At the time that I desidet to represent other manufactures, Original Novelty of Chicago operated a small bussines. I coled them and I told them I am comming over to taulk to them, that I would liked to represent them. They whore very pleasd to see me.

They handled only plastic goods. Braiselets, barettes, combs. Olso imports. But only plastic. Perfect Pearl does not handle plastic so they would not be a competing line.

There whore two partners in the bussines at that time. I closed with them a deal for the intire country. The deal was for me to style, to desighn for them and to buy material to whote I thoght would be the rite thing to manufacture and to sell. In a short time I got them distribution oll over the country. That was manny manny years ago.

Years later the two partners separated. Walter Guttman remained in the bussines by him self. At that time I told Walter I will do oll I can for him and I did, until at present in the later years my son Howard took it over as I could not trevel any more.

Thanks to God Howard and Lloyd are doing an escelent job for Original Novelty at this time of wich I am very proud of my childrn.

*Good luck, Walter.*

## PENNY PENDLETON

How I heppend to get this line to represent oll over the country was a kinney funny insident. It heppend in Providence at the Baltimore Hotel.

I was having lunch at the restaurant. Long side of me there was sitting Irin Miller from Kansas City. In a conversation Irin said to me

—Sami, ther is a manufacture in St Louis. They manufacture spac bends, wich are long chains that attech to lie glesses. I reely dont know thair name. Try to find out because that will be a good line for you. At present they are selling to the ritail trade, but if you will find him you can close a deal for him to the wholesalers of Costume Jewelry.

—O.K. Irin, I said. I shell try.

The next day instad going home I went straid to St Louis. I heppend to know at the May Co. Dept Store a byer in that fild,

Ida Zastrow.

I came to her office.

—Good morning, Ida.

—Sami. Whoet can I do for you?

—Yes. I would liked for you to find someting out for me.

—Yeas, whote is it?

—Ida. Ther is a manifacture that is manifacturing spac bend lie Gless Holders and I know that you are bying from them.

—Yeas, I do, she repleid. And the name is Penny Pendleton.

—Thanks, I said.

The next thing I coled them up and I maid a date to see him the next day.

When I came in, esusual a warem hand shake. I lit up my cigar and I stard tulking to this very fine young men, his name is Harold Shuckman.

—Harold. I understand you are manifacturing Spac Bend.

—Yes, we do.

—Are you the owner?

—No. Mrs Penny, a fine lady, is the owner of this bussines.

—Am I to do bussines with Mrs Penny or with you?

—You will do bussines with me. I am the meneger of the bussines.

—Good, I said. Well, I understand that you selling your merchandise to the ritail trade.

—Yess, I do.

—Harold, how would you like to sell to the wholesaler of the Costume Jewlry, of the intire country?

—That I would like, Harold repleid.

—Fine, I said. Then thers no problem. I can promis you one thing, that in a short wile I shell promote your Product to the wholesalers. It wont take me to long. Only on one condition, for you not to sell to any ritailer.

—If we make a deal, I shell not sell to the ritail traid.

We closed the deal with a contract and you know I capt my promise and Harold capt his.

Oll in oll I have been selling for Harold the Penny Pendleton line for manny manny years now to our mutual satisfaction.

Thanks to you, Irin.

# >36<

## ANOTHER MEMORY

This is olso another incedent that happend in one of my shows in Providence. One of my dear costimers from Detroit, Michigan—not only a good Costimer but olso a Dear Frend to me, a good boy and good nature. He was olways good at the show for 5-6 thousand dollar order . . .

One time he came to the show and he maid apointment for 8 o'clock in the evening that he will look at my line. (Good). I was very happy. I know that he will give a good order.

That evening befor he came to me he told oll the sailesmen from that show that he's got a date with Sami and they should oll watch that he will have lot of fun with Sami.

Heer he comes on time. He walked in my room. I notised oll the boys and som of the girls cam around my door. I closed the dore.

—Well Sami, show me your line.

And I stardet as usual to show the new line. And every number I showed—

—No No. I dont like you sample line. Whoet kind of merchandise is this? I wont by it.

He taulked like this after looking over the hole line, about 500 numbers.

—Whoet is it? I said to him. You main to tell me that you could not find nothing in my line?

No, was the enswer, No. I am sorry . . .

And he stardet to walk out off my room.

—Look, I said. Is ther somting wrong?

My Frend turns right back and puts his two hands on the table and says,

—Well, Sami, whoets new in your line?

By that time I got very engry.

—Yes, I have some new in my line.

You should excuse my expretion, I let my pents down.

—This is my new line.

## 200

*This is my new line*

For a minut he got white. He did not expect my reaction. Then as I was standing olmost in nude he—my costimer and good frend—opend the door. And everybody jumped in my room, the men and the woomen. It was hilaries and lefter . . .

End of my story—my good Frend and a wanderful Costimer came back and plased as usual a five thousand dollar order, and until today he is and olways will be in my hart a good Frend. . . .

# >37<

## LAST CHEPTER OF MY WIFE

In the younger days I Sami useto go away on the road of wich it lasted from 5-6 weeks at the time. I would leave my dear wife and the childrn for that langth of time—I useto think to my self that her job alone with the childrn and to take care of everything was a much harder job than for me to go on the road. The woomens job—to raise four childrn alone with the husband gone for that langth of time was no picknick. Oll I had to do is sell wich I loved. Nothing else. But for my wife her job was undescrible. I hope that this lesson should be to every treveling sailesmen that the wife has the harder job than the sailesmen. Sure, the money maker is the husband. The sailesmen, he is the one who provides for the family and the wife if the one who works at home with the childrn. But that does not make the husband to put a fether in his cap.

No, to my opinion the wife should get more credit for leading the home. The sailesmen when he finishes the day he can rest at nite or wen he is riding the train at nite. But the woomens job is oll day and som time oll nite. This is why I fill that the woomens job is much harder . . . Her job never ends.

Sure the husband has the responsibility of making money. But a wife and mother has the responsibility of raising a family and taken care the proper way of her household with childrn. No Picknick. So Mr Sailesmen thank more so of your wife and family, regardless of how hard you are working.

My own wife Yetta I told you olredy stayd busy with company and cards wile I was away trevling on the road. That was her terepie and I was very happy about it.

But finally one time efter I became olredy a company representative and gave up my own company I came in from the road to find my wife not so happy as usual. She olways had a happy smile on her face. This time she wasnt smiling.

—Honney, whats wrong? I askt her.

—I will tell you later.

I wonderd if ther was any truble or something important. We sitdarent at the table and had our dinner. Later in the evening she broke the news to me that she has got to go to the hospital for an operation.

—Darling, dont worry. Everything will come out for the best. I tried to comfort her the best I knew how.

That nite I dint sleep too well, knowing the kind of operation shes got to go trugh. The next day I took her to hospital. I consolted with the doctor. Naturly he gave me hopes. But after the operation he broke the bad news to me and my dear childrn. One brest must be removed. My dear wife had cancer.

By that time off course oll the children whore grown up. Bernice and Label whore married and naturly understood the trajidy and condition of their Mother and did everything they could to help her. She suffered terrible and went for another operation for a nu discovery that the big scientist Dr Charles Higgins discovered for cancer. This was don at Billings Hospital.

The operation did not help her but let her live a few more years. It was worth trying anything to save her life. The cancer spred and by that time I understood that befor long I will loos my dear wife.

I lost my happy home.

I carried her from one hospital to another and from one convelescent home to another. I useto come to her tweis daylie to feed her lunch and dinner as by her self she wouldnt eat. Nothing was to hard for me to comfort her.

She has been lingering for about five years and the final came to an End. Oll my trying came to an End.

# >38<

## CHEPTER OF MY SECOND MARIDGE

When my first wife Yetta died I tried to keep up my home even though I was alone. The childrn were oll married. I was hoping that I would be able to keep it up but I found myself lost for a wile. Finely I desidet to sell the intire house funitur and to move into a hotel.

I advertized in the paper funitur for sale.

A lady coled up that she would like to by the intire funitur. Good.

I maid a date for her to come to see the funitur. The excuse was that she needet for her perents.

She came over and efter a wile I relized that the moral of that excuse was not to by the funitur. She was looking for a man to get meried.

She wasnt bad looking but quiet younger than I am. In fact half the age of my years. In the main time when I saw that she becomes sirius I said to her

—Younglady, I dont think that would be the rite thing to do for me. You are olmost as young as my childrn and my childrn would be insulted if I meried someone as young as you are.

She wouldnt take no for an enswer. So I coled on her for a date. I came to her perents home to take her out. Whell, it was so excidet from her perents. The mother put oll kinds of goodies on the table and finely we stard going out for the

evening and the mother said to us

—Childrn, go have a good time.

You know whote? I did.

The wind up is I sold the funitur to a second hand diller and I moved to the Sheridan Beach Hotel. Wile I was leaving at the hotel I did lots of thanking about me settling don. You got to be very lucky to find the right compenenship and a partner of your future life. It is not an easy menner.

You are playing a slot mashin and one of a thousand is lucky and the winer gets the Jack Pot. The same thing is the second maridge. You got to be the lucky one to find the right partner into your future life.

In the maintime I new my present wife Rose for the last six months wile I was dating the young lady who came to by the funitur. My hart was olways drowing to her. Regardless that my present wife Rose is six years younger than I am. . . .

In reality I saw my present wife the first time in my dughter Burnises home. She came ther to visit with my dughter with her in low Sadie Hendelmen. They introdust me to her but I never paid atention at that time, as I was to buzy with oll kinds of dates. In fact I had a good time no metter whote. In the main time I was treveling a lot in my bussines and I forgot oll about her.

One evening I was home alone and I was redy to go out again. As I was wolking out from the haus the telephone rang. It was Sadie Hendelman, my dauhters Mother in low.

—Sam, whote are you dooing in the hous alone?

—I am not alone. I was just going out.

—Sam, how about going to a show donton? Mrs Rose Saber is heer. How about comming over? Will oll go to the show.

In the sper of a moment I said

—Good. I will.

I came over to Sadies house and we oll went donton. We went to the Chicago Theatre. In the theatre I was sitting in the midle, Sadie from one side and Rose my present wife on the other side. As it got dark in the theatre I was kind of squizing Roses hand. If you know Sami, he never sits still.

Well, the show was over. I took the two laidies to Fritzels for coffee. Than we went home. First I meneged to take Sadie home, then I took Rosie home. As I stoped neer her house I said.

—Can I coll you?

—Sure, she said. Why not?

—O.K.

She gave me her telephone number, and said good nite and thankt me for the good time we had.

In the main time when Rose went up stairs she coled up Sadie.

—Sadie, tell me. Is Sam your boy frend?

—No Rose. Dont be a fool. He is not my boy frend. And if he will coll you for a date, escept. I will be very heppy if he will coll you from me colling him up. I ment him for you, not me.

In the main time I left for the road. I came back in a couple off weeks and I coled her up. I maid a date for Saterday nite. We went to a show. Then for dinner. Dinner time at the table we were tulking vereas things abot life. Especialy of her own life, of her former meridge and about her childrn.

—How long ago did your husband died?

—About fifteen years ago, Rose replid.

I said

—You ment to tell me soch a beautuful woomen stayd not meried so long? Naturly I supose the rite one did not com along for you.

In returned she smiled at me.

—Yes, you are right. The right one didnt come to me.

By that time it got kind of late. I took her home. I bead her a sweet goot nite and I went to my hotel.

I have been thanking about her. Whote I did liked about her was her behaving and her vocabelery, the way she related to me vereas things about her own life, the way she has rased her own family and whote she went trugh in the days from her own first maridge and the family.

I have been colling on her many times and the more I have been with her I had enjouet more than with anabody else. Her writing and her vocabliry and her behaving maid me closer to her than any other woomen that I have been going out with. In fact wile I have been dating Rose I still have been dating other woomen and having good times with others. But no one came to par as my present wife Rose.

The more I was going out with other woomen the more my present wife became top of them oll. More wisdom. More intelegent. More beautiful. More and more in every way as a laidie. . . .

I shell never forget one evening in her apartment she stardet to get dresst to go out. By exsident not knowing I opend the door from her dressing room and ther she was standing olmost in nud. I got startlet for a moment seeing her beautiful body. She looked to me like an engil in haven. That is the time wen I realy got in love in her.

Yet. I never promised to mery her but in my hart I felt if I will deside to get maried she will be the one. I had been getting propositions from other woomen, money and what-not. Rose my present dear wife didnt have any money. That I knew. But she had posest something in her life that no other woomen had. I knew in my hart that she will make me a good wife, good company, good life and above all a good partner.

Rose had three childrn. Burnie was the oldest. Ell was single. Ellenor was married.

When Burnie became in the age of 15 he took up som music lecence in hy scool and he was pretty good at it. In fact he stardet and orgenized boys from hy scool and maid his own band. He olso took for a wile from a ticher to learn and be a better musition than the rest of the boys from scool. As a young boy he had great idias and maid up his mine to become a leader of an orkestra and have his name on billbords. He demendet from his Mother lots of things—he be drest nise, have a nise home—lots of things his Mother couldnt efort. His Mother did oll she can to raise a fine family and that she did.

In the main time Burnie playd with his band around the naborhood. He playd at moovie houses and som privit partys. He meneged to make a few dollars heer and there. One nite he came home and he said to his Mother

—Mother, I am going with my orcaster on a one nite stand to play.

Mother said to him

—Dont do that, I dont like this. Not for a young men like you comming from a nise family. But if you do dont come home before six months.

Finaly Burnie left with his orcaster. On the way home they didnt have enof money or to eat. They picht in and bought a car for $25.00 and finaly with strogle came home, fell in Mothers home frozen, hungry and whote not. Mother put up som food on the table and fed them all. Later Burnie went to St Louis, played at Chase Hotel with his name advertised, Burnie and the Swordsmen, then to New Orleans, played at Hotel Monte Lion. He came to Chicago and played at the Palmer House and the Blackstone.

In the later years Burnie went to the army and was station in Michigan. He got to be very lonely there. It was no place to go exsept in the bereks. There was nothing to do exsept drill, eat, shine the shoes and sleep.

*Burnie with strogel came home*

Finely they had a dense in that little town and he met up with a morst beautiful girl by the name Edith and befor long Burnie stard keeping company pretty steady. On a Sonday this little girl invited him to the house for dinner and befor long they desidet to get married. Of course Bernie wasnt bad looking either and Edith this beautuful girl so that Burnie possesst som quality that no other boy had. And you know whoet? She didnt made a mistake. They set a date for the weading befor Burnie had to go overseas. Mother and Elenor went to the weading.

From the begining ther was a little misunderstanding but as time went on Edith is considerd by Burnies Mother another dauther. Not a daughter in low.

A few years later thanks God Burnie came home. He stardet to setle down with his musick profashion. One great thing about Burnie—he had ambition and a good hat on his shoulders. And then Edith his wife helpt him a lot. Outside of being a devoted wife she became a lieder in his life. She maid him to quit playing and advised him to stard writing musick and making jingles for vereas companys—for cockola, the

Green Jiints and from then on vereas other companys. To day Burnie became a sucsesful writer in the musick fild and is considerd one of the best.

His family consist of two boys and one girl. The entire family is living in Scottsdale Arizona one happy family together.

The second boy of my dear wife Rose his name is Ell. For a nickname they coll him Babe. He was olways with his Mother. He too studied musick and became one of the best in the musick profashion. In fact the professor from the Musick Caledge wanted him to play on the Simphony Orcester. He playd the Bays Fidel. But Ell did not exsept this. He figert out that in the long run he will make more money to play independently by himsellf and make a better livelihood for the future. And so he did.

His first independent job he playd in the Pomp Room of the Ambasador East Hotel for many years and became knowing as one of the finest in the musick fild. When Ell (Babe) was yunger

**215**

he won a scalership from the Curtis Institute of Musick in Philidelphia.

By nature Ell has been the morst effectunet son and very good nature. Nothing was to hard to do for his Mother and he helpt her in every way. He wasnt ashaime how tired he has been to com home and wash the floor. Oll in oll Babe has been an understanding son.

By the time I Sami stardet to keep company with Rose, I olways found Ell to be good nature. By that time his Mother wanted Babe to settled down but for Babe was very hard to find the right kind of a girl for dates. The only time Ell can have off and have a date is on a Monday because he worked the other nites, aspacialy Saterday and Sonday. So as time went on Babe met up with a girl and told his Mother about her that she was beautuful and more interesting than other girls he met, understanding and from a fine femily. They stardet to keep stedy company and Mother said

—Dont waist no time. If you like her, I sure will like her.

Befor long Mother maid an engagement party in her house and invited oll her frends and the family, my family too. They set a date for the weading. At the weading was just a few frends and the family at the Drake Hotel. Now Babe and Ruth are raizing a beautuful family of their own. Two beautiful little girls, Lisa and Sally.

As a son to his Mother Babe has not changed. No mether how bizy he is he will coll his Mother every day and find time to vizit with her tweis a week.

Roses dauther Elenor greadjeated hi scool with the finest credits. Efter that she took a special course of buckipping and befor long got a job as a buckipper in a office. She new one thing—by beeing a buckipper she will olways have a job and be able to help her Mother. Elenore was petite and beautiful. Her Mother sowd and maid her oll kind of outfits. Her Mother was a good desighner and was able to sow good.

Finely Elenore desidet to get married to a youngmen named Less Davis who just got back from the Army and they dayted for about a year. The Mother maid the weading and now Elenor is heppily married and has a young son named Spenser. In the younger days Spenser was kind of a Wikling. But Elenors help maid him a helthy youngmen. You wont find many Mothers like Elenor. Today Spens finish coledge and wile he went to scool he meneged to work and saft up som monney by working in the Post Office. For Spans nothing was to hard. He is finer than the everich boy on the street and never makes demends on his perents.

In the main time I admired the way Rose has raised her childrn, before we got married. Dooing the time I have been keeping company with her she never yet mention to me of security for her like other women do. She was olways satisfied

Elenou desidet to get merried

with little things. Olways with a smile. Never shoed me any sercazim. Her home was olways neet and clean and she her self was olso dressd neet and stylish. She meneged oll of that with whoetever little money she had. Her best hoby in her life was a good book, and writing, wich I admired about her.

In the main time I was leaving at the Sheridan Beach Hotel, and kept my self buzie working and treveling. When I came back from the road I didnt feel too good in helth. I coled up Dr. Lerner. He was not only a Phisitian he olso was a personal frend of mine. He came over to the hotel and exsement me and said

—Sam, get drest, I will take you to the hospital. You need attention, sombody to make a cope of tea. You are not in position to stay heer alone.

He said he thoght I had numonia. So I went to the hospital

and staed ther a week and got well.

Right ther and then I maid up my mine to get married.

The next Sonday morning I went over to Elenors house and Rose was ther visiting. When I came in I took Roses hand.

—Honney, lets sidaren for a wile.

Then I said

—Next Sonday we are getting married.

I took off my ring from my hand and put it on her finger as a symbol of our maridge. Imediately I let them know my childrn, and Rose coled up her childrn and we told them oll we are getting merried.

I for got to mention one peregraf, that two weeks befor this Rose coled me up on the phone that I need not coll on her again . . . that she desidet not to see me any more and she was trugh thanking of meridge. Well in a way she was right. Keeping company for 2½ years is enoph.

Anyway the weading took place in Burnises home. It went trugh beatuful. We rented a beautuful apt, we mooved in the fowloring week. And you know whoet? My judgment was right, whoet I thoght of my dear wife from the beginning I met her. I find her wanderful the manny years we have been living together, twenty years now. I hopt to the end of our life we should go on as we are—living happy oll of this years. I did not maid a mistake. It took me olmost three years to make this dession. I am not sorry.

The end of the story is that my wifes childrn are happy that thair Mother found good compenionship in her life and my childrn are heppy that I found true and lovely compenenship to prolong my life.

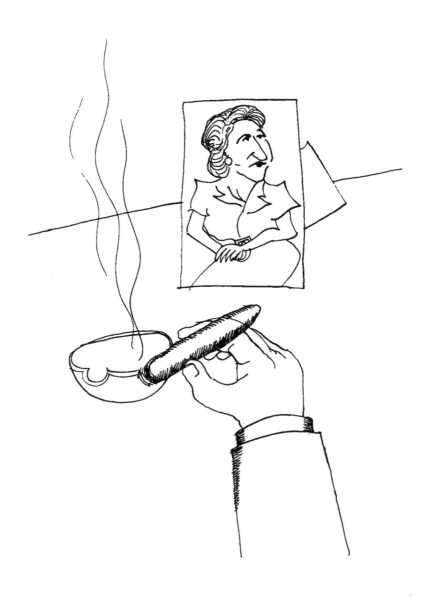

220

# >39<

## HENDLING TOFF SITUASHONS

There are times when a super sailesmen has to com face to face with more than costimers.

Ones going home from my office I uprucht the yellow light crossing the bulvard. I have the right to cross wile the yellow lite is on. Wile I was crossing in the midle of the trafick the light turned to red. Well, I cant go back. So I croset over.

As I was minding my own bussines one block further I see in the mirror that a polis car is right near the back of me blingking at me. This is the sighn to stop, so I did.

The polismen wolked up to me. I opend the window.

—Yeser, anything wrong? I said to him.

This maid him very exsidet and he stardet howloring at me as I became the biggerst criminal.

I opend the car dore and I wolked out.

—Let me have your driving license, he said.

—Yeser, I said, and I gave it to him.

But that polismen never stoped howloring at me, with a very uprobt tone of woice. By that time I thoght to myself, Sami, use your sailesmenship. So I poot my hand on his shulder and I said

—Yes, you have the right to stop me but not to howlor at me. Dont forget I am your costimer. When I coll on a costimer I dont howler on him. I smile on him. Dont forget you are making a leaving from me. So dont get engry, and dont howler on a costimer when you uproch him.

He stopd and lookd at me for a minut. Then he scrached his big had and he said to me

—Mister, I am at this beat for over 20 years and this is the first time I have got that kind of engel from anabody. Go home. Go.

, Another toff situashon arose wans upon the time true my treveling on the road the goverment coled me in to check my treveling expences.

The men that wrought the letter to me cold me into his office.

—Yeser, I said. Mine name is Sam Silverman.

—O yes, he said. Come in, Mr Silverman. I am checking your expence account. It looks to me that there is a little bid to much heer. Will you kindly explaine to me about this expence account.

—Yesser, I will. But must I explaine to you now?

—No, Mr Silverman, take your time. The goverment has plenty time. Come in when you are redy.

—O.K. Then I shell come in towmorow.

—Very vell. Any time.

The next day I pact up three large sample cases with oll my lines that I represent. I hired a men, strong, and he helpt me to weel in oll my sample cases to the goverment office.

When we came in with oll the cases than the goverment men said to me

—Whoets oll this?

—Yesser, I said. I broght in my evidents to you, my dear sir, regarding my inormas expens account that you wish to know,

—Oh yes, he said. Lets see.

—Well, this is to show you the way I trevel. With three sample cases and olso my personal bag you must have Porter

**223**

and Cab. Olso when you coll on a costimer you must have help to carry the sample cases. You olso must understand the kind of help you get they cant hardly sighn ther name. Ther is no resipt to get, and I pay him from twelve to fifteen dollars a day out side of the cabs that I use dooing the day and the cab men in morst cases dont give you a resept. I hope you reilised by now my inormas Expens.

—You are right, Mr Silverman, the goverment men said. You can go. You wont be botherd again.

—Thank you, Sair, I said.

So ther again I had to use my sailesmenship.

# >40<

## CHEPTER ABOUT RETIERMENT

Thousand of people get fired from ther jobs in the age of 62. This is wrong and should never be permited by the goverment. This people become a vegetable and a detrement to the sociede of wich they live on the Social Security for the rest of there life. On the other hand the goverment tells them

—You stay home and we will take care of you for the rest of your life.

Som of the people are very happy. Sure they can have a good time. Why not? They can stay home and live of the fat of the land witout dooing anathing. But you will find morst people are at a loss. At 62 they are healthy, good mynde, strong physicly—wolking around the streets trying to find whoet to do. And no one wanst to give him or her a job to keep them happy. They would be very happy to pay the goverment texas on ther aditional extra income. That wont do.

—You are too old. Sorry, you are over 62.

Let me tell you that in my 85 years of experence I have met manny thousand of people in ther 62 and over, that ther mind and wisdom are much more superior to any young men finishing colledge in the ages 25 years and over. When they finish they dont no how to face the world with oll thair education. Now my advise is, open up the doors for him or she over the age 62. Wright to the Supreme Court to exsapt people over 62 to give them jobs. That alone to my mind would change the econimy in this golden land of America.

Now I have to add this advise to young or old. Do not retire. Retierment shortins your life. And you become a vegetible the rest of your life. Just becouse sombody is bogging in your ear to retier as we have enoph money for the rest of our life.

—We have enoph to leave on. We dont need any more. Lets enjoie our life.

THATS WRONG. Dont retiyer. As long as you can heer, tolk and wolk and are rizonably helthy, keep yourself bizy.

227

You can shorten your hours to limatation 4-5 hours a day *but dont retird.* Atend to your bussines in the morning and the rest of the day get your self som hoby. Resting. Play a little cards. Play gulf. Play jean romey or else if you like exsitement love up to your wife or sombody else. Do it. Dont neglected. *Do it.*

Againe I repid dont shorten your life by retierment. As long as you helth permit you keep up working. Keep your self bizy. Unless your helth dont permit you. This is someting else.

By fowloring my advise, you will prolong your life for manny manny years. Another advise I shell give you. When you finish your morning work go home to your wife, enjoie the rest of the day. Or if you havnt anybody home you are alone, get your self a frend. That will olso give you inspiration to go on.

Dont stay home alone.

Get out from the house in the morning. You are only in somebodys way. Monny dont make happiness. It helps . . . But no metter if you make monney that day or not go out and mingle in the world with people. To get up in the morning having breakfast, then waite for lunch, then wait for dinner— that is defintly not a happy life.

I olso advise that wacation you should take. But short trips, 2-3 weeks, every so often, every once in a wiele. That will olso bring you memories and happines.

This is my last advise to oll of yous. From a old old expirence in life.

S.S.

228